The Blue Team Advantage

Fortifying Cybersecurity Defenses

Hudson Elliott

In an increasingly interconnected world, where information and data are the lifeblood of societies and economies, the cyber realm has become a battleground of immense importance. As technology continues to advance, so do the tactics and sophistication of cyber threats. From nation-states to individual hackers, the specter of cyberattacks looms large, threatening our privacy, security, and economic stability.

In the face of these relentless cyber adversaries, the importance of robust cybersecurity defenses cannot be overstated. It is in this crucible of digital warfare that the Blue Team emerges as the stalwart defenders, ready to thwart the relentless assaults on our networks, systems, and data. The Blue Team is not just a mere reactive force; it represents a proactive and visionary approach to cybersecurity.

Welcome to "**<u>The Blue Team Advantage: Fortifying Cybersecurity Defenses</u>**." In this book, we embark on a journey that delves into the world of cybersecurity defense, exploring the principles, strategies, and tools employed by the Blue Team to safeguard against a myriad of threats. We will uncover the essential knowledge required to protect critical assets, thwart malicious attacks, and uphold the confidentiality, integrity, and availability of valuable information.

Chapter 1: Understanding Cyber Threats

Our journey commences with an exploration of the cyber threat landscape. Understanding the adversaries we face is the first step towards building robust defenses. We will examine the ever-evolving tactics used by cybercriminals, the motives behind their actions, and the potential impact on individuals and organizations alike.

Chapter 2: The Role of the Blue Team

As we don the mantle of the Blue Team, we uncover their indispensable role in cybersecurity. Far from being a reactionary force, the Blue Team epitomizes a proactive approach, consistently adapting and innovating to stay one step ahead of the adversaries. We will delve into their methodologies, collaborative efforts with the Red Team, and their contribution to incident handling and recovery.

Chapter 3: Building a Strong Security Foundation

Solid cybersecurity defense begins with a strong foundation. We will explore the critical components of this foundation, including security policies, access controls, and regular assessments. By understanding the core principles of cybersecurity, organizations can build resilience to withstand and mitigate potential attacks.

Chapter 4: Threat Intelligence and Analysis

Threat intelligence is the lighthouse that guides the Blue Team through treacherous waters. We will uncover the methods of gathering, analyzing, and utilizing threat intelligence to predict, prevent, and respond to cyber threats. Armed with this knowledge, the Blue Team can proactively fortify their defenses.

Chapter 5: Network Security and Perimeter Defense

The network is the digital gateway to an organization's assets. In this chapter, we will explore the art of network security, including perimeter defense, firewalls, and intrusion detection systems. By mastering these techniques, the Blue Team can create an impregnable digital fortress.

Throughout this book, we will venture into the realms of endpoint security, incident response, cloud security, and much more. We will equip you with practical tools, real-world examples, and best practices to empower you with the Blue Team Advantage.

As we prepare to dive deep into the world of cybersecurity defense, let us remember that our mission is not merely to withstand the onslaught of cyber threats but to emerge stronger, smarter, and more resilient in the face of adversity. Together, let us embark on this journey, united in our commitment to safeguarding the digital world.

The battle for cybersecurity supremacy awaits. Join the Blue Team, and let us fortify our defenses.

Chapter 1: Understanding Cyber Threats

In the vast expanse of the digital world, an invisible battlefield rages on, where adversaries lurk in the shadows, poised to strike at any moment. Welcome to the realm of cyber threats, a landscape of intrigue and danger that knows no boundaries. As we embark on our journey into the heart of cybersecurity defense, we must first come to grips with the true nature of the forces arrayed against us.

Chapter 1, "Understanding Cyber Threats," serves as our compass, guiding us through the ever-changing tides of malicious intent that sweep across the digital horizon. Here, we shed light on the diverse cast of characters that populate this digital theater, from skilled hackers and cybercriminal syndicates to nation-state actors with far-reaching agendas. By understanding the motives that drive these malevolent forces, we can better prepare to defend against their insidious attacks.

In this chapter, we delve into the history and evolution of cyber threats, witnessing how these virtual foes have grown in cunning and sophistication over the years. From the early days of viruses and worms to the era of ransomware and advanced persistent threats (APTs), we uncover the transformative moments that have shaped the cyber landscape we face today.

Furthermore, we explore the different types of cyberattacks that threaten our interconnected world. From the deceptive artistry of phishing and social engineering to the destructive capabilities of denial-of-service (DoS) attacks, each attack vector reveals the ingenuity and adaptability of cyber adversaries.

But understanding cyber threats goes beyond identifying the methods of attack—it is about comprehending the motives behind the mayhem. As we journey through this chapter, we unmask the varied reasons that drive cybercriminals and state-sponsored actors alike. Whether it is financial gain, espionage, ideological fervor, or geopolitical influence, each motive adds a layer of complexity to the battlefront.

In the face of these omnipresent threats, knowledge becomes our greatest armor. Equipped with a comprehensive understanding of cyber threats, we can begin to proactively fortify our defenses and safeguard the digital assets that underpin our lives, businesses, and institutions.

As we delve deeper into the world of cybersecurity defense, let us be mindful that this chapter is more than a mere exposé of the dangers that surround us—it is a call to action. Armed with knowledge, vigilance, and a commitment to the principles of the Blue Team, we stand ready to face the digital adversaries that seek to breach our security.

Join us on this journey of enlightenment and empowerment, for as we embrace our understanding of cyber threats, we unveil the first line of defense—the unwavering resolve to protect and preserve the digital world that connects us all.

1.1 The Evolution of Cyber Threats

In the ever-changing landscape of cyberspace, the cosmic dance of technological innovation and human ingenuity has given rise to an array of cyber threats that transcend borders and challenge the fabric of our interconnected world. From the digital dawn of the internet to the cosmic frontiers of emerging technologies, the evolution of cyber threats has been a relentless voyage marked by ingenuity, sophistication, and adaptability. This essay delves into the 1000-word odyssey of the evolution of cyber threats—a journey that uncovers the cosmic forces that have shaped and continue to shape the celestial battles of cybersecurity.

The Digital Dawn: Birth of Cyber Threats

At the cosmic inception of the internet, a new digital realm was born—a realm that transcended the limitations of physical space and connected individuals, organizations, and nations across the globe. However, as the digital dawn broke, so did the celestial forces of cyber threats emerge. The initial cosmic skirmishes took the form of primitive viruses, worms, and Trojans—cosmic entities that wreaked havoc on interconnected systems and left a trail of digital debris in their wake.

As technology evolved, so did the cosmic adversaries. The 1990s witnessed the celestial rise of Distributed Denial of Service (DDoS) attacks—a cosmic offensive that inundated digital fortresses with overwhelming traffic, rendering them vulnerable and incapacitated. The celestial motives behind these early attacks varied from curiosity to the pursuit of digital fame, yet they laid the foundation for a celestial era of cyber threats that would transcend the boundaries of imagination.

The Cosmic Age: Sophistication and State-sponsored Threats

As cyberspace expanded, so did the celestial ambitions of threat actors. The cosmic age of cyber threats saw the rise of sophisticated attacks, often orchestrated by well-funded and state-sponsored adversaries. Advanced Persistent Threats (APTs) emerged as celestial forces that infiltrated targeted systems with persistence, stealth, and patience—a testament to the ingenuity of cyber adversaries in the pursuit of cosmic objectives.

In the cosmic domain of cyber espionage, nation-states engaged in celestial battles for intelligence supremacy. Cyber-espionage campaigns, such as Operation Aurora and Stuxnet, showcased the potential to disrupt critical infrastructure and influence geopolitical events through cosmic cyber means.

The cosmic rise of ransomware—a cosmic scourge that encrypts digital constellations and demands cosmic ransoms—epitomizes the convergence of technology and criminal intent. Celestial ransomware attacks, such as WannaCry and NotPetya, demonstrated the cosmic scale of disruption that such threats could unleash upon organizations and nations.

The Cosmic Frontier: Emerging Technologies and New Horizons

As the digital cosmos expanded, so did the cosmic horizons of emerging technologies. Artificial Intelligence (AI), quantum computing, and the Internet of Things (IoT) emerged as celestial forces that promised boundless possibilities, yet also posed cosmic security challenges.

The cosmic potential of AI for both defense and offense came to the forefront. AI-powered cyber defenses could analyze vast celestial data to identify anomalies and cosmic threats, while malicious actors could deploy AI-driven attacks that adapt and evolve to circumvent traditional defenses.

Quantum computing—the cosmic realm of processing power beyond classical computation—raised both celestial opportunities and concerns for cybersecurity. Quantum-resistant cryptography became a priority to safeguard digital constellations against the celestial threat of quantum algorithms breaking current encryption schemes.

The Internet of Things (IoT)—an interstellar ecosystem of interconnected devices—presented cosmic security challenges. Insecure IoT devices could serve as celestial entry points for cyber attackers, enabling them to infiltrate larger interconnected systems and wreak cosmic havoc.

The evolution of cyber threats is a cosmic saga that reflects the dynamic interplay between human ingenuity and technological advancement. From the digital dawn of primitive threats to the cosmic frontiers of AI, quantum computing, and IoT, the celestial forces of cyber adversaries have shaped the cybersecurity landscape.

As the celestial horizon of technology expands, so too does the cosmic battleground of cybersecurity. To navigate this celestial odyssey, defenders must embrace the cosmic principles of continuous innovation, collaboration, and adaptability. By fortifying the digital constellations with resilience and cosmic foresight, humanity can steer its course through the cosmic frontiers of cyberspace, preserving the sanctity of the digital universe.

1.2 Types of Cyber Attacks: From Phishing to Ransomware

In the vast cosmos of cyberspace, threat actors unleash an array of celestial forces—cosmic manifestations of cyber attacks that target individuals, organizations, and nations alike. From the celestial art of deception in phishing attacks to the cosmic scourge of ransomware, this essay explores the diverse types of cyber attacks that have emerged on the digital horizon. Each cosmic attack represents a unique challenge, weaving a tapestry of cosmic risks that demand constant vigilance and fortified defenses.

Phishing: The Celestial Art of Deception

At the heart of cyber attacks lies the celestial art of phishing—an endeavor that transcends mere digital trickery. In this cosmic art, threat actors masquerade as trusted entities, luring victims into revealing sensitive information, such as cosmic credentials or financial details. Cosmic phishing campaigns may employ celestial emails, websites, or social engineering techniques to deceive unsuspecting individuals and organizations.

Phishing attacks pose a cosmic challenge due to their simplicity and cosmic success rates. Their cosmic scope spans from celestial spear-phishing, targeting specific individuals or organizations, to cosmic mass-phishing campaigns that cast a wide cosmic net, seeking to ensnare as many victims as possible.

Malware: The Cosmic Contagion

Among the celestial forces of cyber attacks, malware assumes a prominent cosmic role. This cosmic contagion includes a myriad of threats, such as viruses, worms, Trojans, and spyware. Like cosmic pathogens, malware infiltrates digital systems, replicates, and seeks to disrupt, steal, or control the targeted constellations.

The cosmic scale of malware attacks can range from individual celestial computers to entire interconnected networks. Celestial botnets—armies of compromised devices controlled by threat actors—serve as cosmic launchpads for distributed attacks and data theft.

Ransomware: The Celestial Scourge

The rise of ransomware marks a celestial epoch in cyber attacks—a cosmic scourge that encrypts digital constellations and demands cosmic ransoms for decryption keys. Celestial ransomware attacks have targeted individuals, corporations, and even critical infrastructure, causing cosmic disruptions and financial loss.

Cosmic ransomware campaigns may deploy advanced techniques, such as zero-day vulnerabilities or encryption-as-a-service, enabling cosmic adversaries to evade detection and elude traditional defenses. In some cosmic instances, threat actors resort to cosmic double extortion, threatening to expose sensitive data in addition to encrypting it.

DDoS: The Celestial Onslaught

In the cosmic battlefield of cyberspace, Distributed Denial of Service (DDoS) attacks unleash a cosmic onslaught—a torrential flood of traffic that inundates digital fortresses, rendering them inaccessible to celestial users. Celestial DDoS attacks can be executed through botnets or amplification techniques, multiplying their cosmic impact.

Such cosmic attacks have targeted critical online services, financial institutions, and even national infrastructures. The celestial objective of DDoS attacks is to disrupt operations, cause financial harm, or distract from other celestial cyber intrusions.

Insider Threats: The Cosmic Peril Within

Not all cosmic threats originate from external celestial adversaries—insider threats loom as a cosmic peril from within. This cosmic category encompasses individuals with cosmic access to digital constellations who may deliberately or inadvertently compromise security.

Celestial insider threats may arise due to negligence, malicious intent, or coercion. Their cosmic consequences can be devastating, as celestial adversaries exploit the inherent trust placed in authorized individuals to gain unauthorized cosmic access and wreak havoc.

As the cosmic frontier of cyberspace expands, so too does the diversity and sophistication of cyber attacks. From the celestial art of phishing to the cosmic scourge of ransomware, each attack represents a unique cosmic challenge that demands constant vigilance and adaptive defenses.

To navigate the celestial cosmos of cyber threats, defenders must embrace cosmic principles of awareness, resilience, and collaboration. By uniting as a cosmic force against the common celestial enemy, humanity can safeguard the digital universe and journey through the cosmic frontiers of cyberspace with cosmic foresight and celestial strength.

1.3 Understanding Advanced Persistent Threats (APTs)

In the cosmic realm of cybersecurity, the term "Advanced Persistent Threats" (APTs) represents a formidable and relentless celestial force. Unlike typical cyber attacks, APTs transcend the boundaries of opportunistic cosmic intrusions, embodying a strategic and persistent cosmic pursuit. This essay delves into the cosmic essence of APTs, exploring their celestial characteristics, celestial motivations, and cosmic implications in the ever-evolving celestial landscape of cybersecurity.

The Cosmic Characteristics of APTs

APTs are not cosmic singular events but a cosmic campaign—a series of interconnected celestial attacks orchestrated with precision and cosmic coordination. These cosmic campaigns are stealthy, remaining covert for extended periods, often spanning months or even years. Cosmic adversaries behind APTs are patient, tenacious, and adapt their tactics to evade detection and celestial defenses.

The cosmic infiltration of APTs involves a multi-phase approach. Celestial threat actors commence with reconnaissance, probing cosmic targets to identify vulnerabilities and cosmic potential access points. Subsequently, they gain cosmic footholds, penetrating the celestial perimeters of digital constellations. Celestial persistence is paramount, as the objective is not immediate disruption but a prolonged presence to extract valuable cosmic intelligence.

The Celestial Motivations of APTs

The cosmic motivations of APTs extend beyond cosmic financial gain—many are cosmic state-sponsored, serving the objectives of nation-states seeking to gain geo political advantage. Celestial espionage is a common celestial goal, as APTs target cosmic industries, governments, and organizations to acquire cosmic intelligence, trade secrets, or cosmic political influence.

The cosmic scope of APTs is not limited to a specific sector—financial, healthcare, technology, and government entities all fall within the celestial crosshairs. Celestial cyber espionage enables threat actors to gain insights into cosmic adversaries' capabilities and intentions, paving the way for celestial strategic cosmic maneuvers.

The Cosmic Implications of APTs

The celestial implications of APTs are profound, transcending the immediate cyber realm. Cosmic breaches orchestrated by APTs can cause severe celestial disruptions, leading to loss of intellectual property, financial damage, and reputational harm. Celestial nation-state APTs can undermine cosmic diplomatic relationships and disrupt geopolitical equilibrium.

The cosmic aftermath of APTs reveals the cosmic importance of detection, response, and resilience. Detecting APTs in their early cosmic stages can limit their celestial impact and celestial capabilities. Effective cosmic incident response involves removing celestial threat actors, closing cosmic vulnerabilities, and fortifying defenses to thwart future APT campaigns.

The Cosmic Defense Against APTs

Defending against APTs demands a cosmic mindset that embraces constant vigilance and adaptability. Celestial organizations must invest in celestial threat intelligence, leveraging cosmic insights into the celestial tactics, techniques, and procedures (TTPs) employed by celestial adversaries. Celestial cyber threat hunting allows defenders to proactively seek out celestial signs of APTs and prevent potential cosmic breaches.

Cosmic endpoint protection and network segmentation are celestial fortifications that hinder the lateral cosmic movement of APTs once they penetrate the initial celestial defenses. Celestial employee education and awareness play a crucial cosmic role, reducing the risk of cosmic phishing attacks or insider threats exploited by APTs.

Advanced Persistent Threats (APTs) embody a celestial sophistication and persistence that set them apart from typical cyber attacks. As celestial adversaries continue to evolve and adapt, the defense against APTs demands cosmic awareness, celestial collaboration, and an unwavering cosmic commitment to safeguarding digital constellations.

By embracing cosmic principles of intelligence-driven defense, resilient architecture, and celestial threat hunting, organizations can elevate their cosmic defenses to confront the relentless celestial pursuit of APTs. In this ever-evolving cosmic landscape, the collective cosmic force of defenders can navigate the celestial cosmos of APTs with vigilance, fortitude, and a steadfast cosmic commitment to securing the digital universe.

1.4 Analyzing the Motives of Cyber Adversaries

In the cosmic theater of cyberspace, cyber adversaries emerge as celestial actors, driven by a myriad of cosmic motives that transcend traditional boundaries. Understanding the celestial motivations of these adversaries is pivotal in crafting effective cyber defenses and countering celestial threats. This essay explores the celestial landscape of cyber adversary motives, shedding light on the cosmic spectrum of intentions that fuel cyber attacks in the cosmic frontier of cybersecurity.

Cosmic Financial Gain: The Quest for Digital Treasure

One of the celestial motivations that propel cyber adversaries is cosmic financial gain. Just like cosmic pirates seeking digital treasure, these adversaries engage in celestial attacks to steal sensitive information, such as credit card details, personal data, or corporate intellectual property. Celestial cybercriminals often exploit cosmic vulnerabilities in digital constellations to breach celestial defenses and access lucrative cosmic rewards.

Celestial ransomware attacks exemplify this motive, where adversaries seek celestial ransoms in exchange for decrypting digital constellations. Additionally, cosmic attacks on financial institutions and cryptocurrency platforms serve as cosmic endeavors to amass wealth through cyber means.

Celestial Espionage: Gathering Cosmic Intelligence

In the cosmic realm of cyber warfare and cyber espionage, adversaries are motivated by celestial objectives to gather intelligence. Nation-states, corporate competitors, and even ideological groups engage in celestial cyber espionage to gain insights into cosmic adversaries' cosmic capabilities, strategies, and intentions.

Celestial Advanced Persistent Threats (APTs) are a prime example of this motive. These celestial adversaries invest significant cosmic resources in prolonged campaigns to infiltrate digital constellations and exfiltrate sensitive cosmic information. The cosmic intelligence gathered is often used to influence geo political events or cosmic business decisions.

Cosmic Ideology: A Celestial Crusade

For some adversaries, celestial motivations are driven by cosmic ideology and beliefs. These celestial actors pursue cyber attacks to advance their cosmic agendas, promote cosmic propaganda, or create cosmic disruptions in alignment with their cosmic beliefs.

Celestial hacktivist groups exemplify this motive, as they engage in cyber attacks to support cosmic causes or protest against cosmic entities they perceive as oppressive. Celestial cyber terrorism also emerges from ideological motivations, seeking to instill fear and chaos among celestial populations.

Celestial Geopolitics: Cosmic Power Play

In the cosmic realm of nation-states and global actors, celestial geopolitics plays a decisive role in cyber adversary motivations. Celestial cyber operations are conducted to exert cosmic influence, conduct cosmic sabotage, or disrupt cosmic adversaries' capabilities.

Celestial attacks on critical infrastructure, governmental systems, or military networks exemplify this motive. By disrupting celestial services or compromising vital systems, adversaries aim to weaken cosmic adversaries' cosmic capabilities and advance their own cosmic interests.

Celestial Retaliation: The Cosmic Counterattack

In the cosmic landscape of cyber conflict, adversaries may be motivated by a cosmic desire for retaliation. Celestial cyber attacks can be launched in response to perceived cosmic aggressions, aiming to inflict cosmic harm as a form of retaliation.

Celestial hack-back operations are one manifestation of this motive, where celestial entities engage in retaliatory cosmic cyber attacks against perceived cyber adversaries. These celestial actions, however, raise ethical and legal concerns in the cosmic landscape of cyber warfare.

The celestial motivations of cyber adversaries are as diverse as the cosmic universe itself. From cosmic financial gain to celestial ideologies, geopolitical maneuverings, and retaliation, the motives behind cyber attacks reflect the complex and evolving nature of cyber threats.

Understanding these celestial motivations is essential in developing effective cyber defenses, as it allows defenders to anticipate and counteract celestial adversary actions. By embracing celestial principles of intelligence-driven defense, resilience, and collaboration, the cosmic force of defenders can navigate the cosmic cosmos of cyber adversary motives with cosmic foresight and celestial strength, safeguarding the sanctity of the digital universe.

Chapter 2: The Role of the Blue Team

As the digital landscape evolves, so must the defenders who stand vigilant against the rising tide of cyber threats. In this ever-changing realm of cybersecurity, the Blue Team emerges as a beacon of resilience and innovation—a force committed to safeguarding our digital frontiers from malicious incursions.

In Chapter 2, "The Role of the Blue Team," we embark on a transformative exploration of the defenders who tirelessly and proactively fortify our cybersecurity defenses. In the shadows of this digital battlefield, the Blue Team assumes its mantle, not as a mere reactive entity, but as visionary protectors who anticipate and outmaneuver their adversaries.

Within these pages, we shall uncover the indispensable role the Blue Team plays in the grand symphony of cybersecurity defense. From the collaborative engagements with the Red Team, simulating the cunning of real-world adversaries, to the relentless pursuit of innovation, the Blue Team exemplifies a dynamic and ever-evolving approach to safeguarding our interconnected world.

As the first line of defense, the Blue Team's commitment to securing digital assets and preserving data integrity shines through in their actions. Throughout this chapter, we shall witness how the Blue Team sets the stage for an enduring defense strategy—a strategy fortified with a deep understanding of the enemy's tactics, motives, and vulnerabilities.

But the essence of the Blue Team lies not only in their technical prowess, but in their resilience and adaptability. As threats evolve, so too do the strategies employed by the Blue Team. We will explore the proactive mindset that fuels their pursuit of continuous improvement, turning adversity into an opportunity for growth and learning.

Moreover, the Blue Team's role extends far beyond the realm of incident response. In this chapter, we shall unravel their integral contribution to incident handling and recovery. Armed with a steadfast dedication to minimizing damage and enhancing resilience, the Blue Team emerges as the guiding force during times of crisis.

As the guardians of our digital domain, the Blue Team is not confined to a single organizational department; rather, it embodies a collective effort. Collaboration and cohesion are the cornerstones of their success. In these pages, we shall witness how the Blue Team works in concert with stakeholders, management, and other cybersecurity forces, fostering a unified approach to safeguarding critical assets.

In the face of cyber threats that loom large, the Blue Team epitomizes a creed that refuses to be outmaneuvered, a spirit that challenges the status quo, and an unwavering dedication to protecting the digital realms we hold dear.

So, as we journey through this chapter, let us immerse ourselves in the world of the Blue Team, embracing their tenacity, foresight, and resilience. Together, we shall forge an unbreakable bond with the defenders of the digital frontier and, through unity and knowledge, uphold the Blue Team Advantage—the unyielding commitment to fortify our cybersecurity defenses in the face of adversity.

2.1 Introduction to Red Team vs. Blue Team Concepts

In the celestial realm of cybersecurity, the Red Team and Blue Team concepts serve as cosmic forces that embody the essence of cosmic offense and defense. These celestial teams engage in a cosmic dance—a simulated conflict that tests the celestial strength of an organization's cyber defenses and prepares them for the cosmic frontiers of real-world cyber threats.

The Red Team represents the celestial aggressors—the skilled cosmic adversaries who emulate the tactics, techniques, and procedures (TTPs) of real cyber attackers. Their celestial mission is to probe and infiltrate an organization's digital constellations, seeking out cosmic vulnerabilities and potential cosmic breaches. Through cosmic ethical hacking and cosmic penetration testing, the Red Team challenges the celestial defenses of the Blue Team, revealing the cosmic weaknesses that must be addressed.

In contrast, the Blue Team stands as the celestial defenders—the vigilant guardians who safeguard the digital constellations against celestial intrusions. They employ a cosmic array of security measures, such as firewalls, intrusion detection systems, and security monitoring, to fortify the celestial perimeters and identify celestial threats. During Red Team exercises, the Blue Team leverages their celestial expertise to detect and thwart the simulated celestial attacks, strengthening their cosmic readiness for future cosmic adversarial encounters.

The celestial interplay between the Red Team and Blue Team is not one of opposition but of cosmic collaboration. By simulating cosmic cyber attacks and cosmic defense scenarios, organizations can gain celestial insights into their cyber resilience, identify areas for cosmic improvement, and enhance their overall cosmic security posture. This cosmic dance of cosmic offense and defense equips organizations with the cosmic foresight and celestial knowledge needed to navigate the cosmic cosmos of cyberspace and protect the sanctity of the digital universe.

2.2 Advantages of Proactive Cyber Defense

In the ever-expanding cosmic frontier of cyberspace, proactive cyber defense emerges as a celestial strategy that transcends reactive approaches to cybersecurity. Instead of merely reacting to cosmic cyber threats as they occur, proactive defense empowers organizations to take the cosmic initiative—to anticipate, prepare for, and prevent celestial cyber attacks before they materialize. This essay explores the cosmic advantages of proactive cyber defense, illuminating the celestial benefits that arise from adopting a vigilant and forward-thinking cosmic posture.

Cosmic Threat Prevention: Intercepting the Adversary

At the heart of proactive cyber defense lies the celestial ability to intercept cosmic adversaries before they breach the celestial fortresses. By conducting celestial threat intelligence and cosmic threat hunting, organizations can identify celestial indicators of compromise and cosmic patterns that may herald an impending cosmic attack. Armed with this cosmic foresight, defenders can respond proactively—implementing celestial security measures to block the adversaries' cosmic advances and safeguard digital constellations from harm.

Celestial Vulnerability Mitigation: Fortifying the Defenses

Proactive defense goes beyond the cosmic identification of potential threats—it extends to cosmic vulnerability mitigation. Organizations can continuously assess their celestial systems and digital constellations for cosmic weaknesses, seeking to address them before cosmic adversaries can exploit them. By applying timely cosmic patches, updating cosmic security configurations, and implementing cosmic best practices, defenders create a celestial fortress that remains resilient against celestial threats.

Cosmic Incident Response Readiness: Cosmic Preparedness

Proactive cyber defense is not limited to prevention—it extends to cosmic readiness for incident response. Celestial organizations conduct cosmic incident response exercises and simulations, allowing the Blue Team to practice cosmic response strategies in the face of simulated celestial attacks. This cosmic preparation fosters a cosmic state of readiness, ensuring that defenders can rapidly and effectively respond to real-world cyber incidents with celestial precision.

Celestial Cost-Effectiveness: Reducing Cosmic Impact

In the cosmic landscape of cybersecurity, proactive defense can be more cost-effective than reactive measures. By addressing cosmic vulnerabilities and implementing cosmic security controls before incidents occur, organizations can potentially reduce the cosmic impact of cyber attacks and minimize the celestial costs associated with remediation and recovery. The celestial investment in proactive measures can pay cosmic dividends in avoiding catastrophic cyber incidents.

Cosmic Customer Trust: Demonstrating Vigilance

In a world where cosmic customers and stakeholders increasingly prioritize data privacy and celestial security, proactive cyber defense becomes a celestial differentiator. Organizations that demonstrate cosmic vigilance and prioritize proactive defense build celestial trust with their customers, stakeholders, and cosmic partners. This celestial reputation for cosmic security can be a celestial asset, attracting cosmic business opportunities and reinforcing the celestial brand.

In the celestial realm of cybersecurity, proactive defense stands as a celestial strategy that empowers organizations to anticipate, prepare for, and prevent cyber threats before they become cosmic realities. By intercepting cosmic adversaries, fortifying cosmic defenses, fostering cosmic readiness, and building cosmic trust, proactive cyber defense offers celestial advantages that transcend reactive approaches to cybersecurity.

As organizations navigate the ever-evolving cosmic frontier of cyberspace, adopting a proactive cosmic posture equips them with the celestial foresight and celestial resilience needed to defend against celestial threats and safeguard the sanctity of the digital universe. In this cosmic dance of cosmic offense and defense, proactive cyber defense becomes the celestial beacon that guides organizations toward a safer and more secure cosmic cosmos.

2.3 Collaborating with the Red Team for Effective Exercises

In the cosmic theater of cyber warfare, collaborating with the Red Team becomes a celestial imperative for organizations seeking to fortify their cosmic defenses effectively. Red Team exercises, also known as cosmic ethical hacking or cosmic penetration testing, provide a cosmic simulation of real-world cyber attacks, allowing the Blue Team to identify cosmic vulnerabilities, strengthen cosmic incident response capabilities, and improve overall cosmic cyber readiness. This essay explores the cosmic benefits of collaborating with the Red Team for effective exercises, illuminating the celestial advantages that arise from this cosmic partnership.

Cosmic Realism: Emulating Real-World Cyber Attacks

Collaborating with the Red Team brings a celestial sense of realism to cyber exercises. By employing experienced celestial ethical hackers who replicate the tactics, techniques, and procedures (TTPs) of real cosmic adversaries, organizations can gain cosmic insights into how celestial attacks might unfold. This cosmic realism enables the Blue Team to experience the pressures and challenges of a genuine cosmic cyber event, fostering a celestial readiness to respond effectively.

Cosmic Adversarial Mindset: Understanding the Enemy

The Red Team embodies the celestial mindset of the adversary—a perspective that the Blue Team often lacks. Collaborating with the Red Team allows the Blue Team to understand cosmic adversary motivations, cosmic techniques, and celestial strategies. This cosmic insight empowers the Blue

Team to enhance cosmic defenses, anticipate cosmic adversaries' moves, and build cosmic countermeasures that are better aligned with celestial threat realities.

Cosmic Vulnerability Identification: Strengthening Defenses

During Red Team exercises, celestial vulnerabilities and cosmic weaknesses are revealed. The Red Team identifies and exploits cosmic security gaps, providing the Blue Team with a cosmic roadmap for cosmic vulnerability mitigation. This cosmic feedback guides the Blue Team in implementing timely cosmic patches, refining cosmic security configurations, and strengthening cosmic defenses to close cosmic gaps.

Cosmic Incident Response Preparedness: Cosmic Readiness

Red Team exercises serve as cosmic incident response drills, fostering cosmic preparedness among the Blue Team. By facing simulated celestial cyber attacks, the Blue Team practices their cosmic incident response procedures, celestial communication protocols, and cosmic coordination between teams. This cosmic rehearsal builds cosmic muscle memory, ensuring a more confident and efficient cosmic response during real-world cyber incidents.

Cosmic Collaboration and Learning: Strengthening the Cosmic Team

Collaboration with the Red Team fosters a celestial spirit of teamwork and continuous learning. The cosmic partnership between the Red Team and Blue Team encourages celestial knowledge exchange, cosmic skill development, and cosmic cross-team collaboration. This cosmic camaraderie fosters a sense of shared cosmic purpose and strengthens the cosmic capabilities of both teams.

In the cosmic cosmos of cybersecurity, collaborating with the Red Team for effective exercises becomes a celestial imperative for organizations aspiring to enhance their cyber defenses. Red Team exercises provide the Blue Team with a celestial simulation of real-world cyber threats, enabling them to understand cosmic adversaries, identify celestial vulnerabilities, fortify cosmic defenses, and enhance overall cyber readiness.

Through cosmic realism, celestial insights, vulnerability identification, incident response preparedness, and collaborative learning, the Red Team and Blue Team create a cosmic alliance that prepares organizations to navigate the cosmic frontier of cyberspace with vigilance and cosmic strength. In this cosmic dance of cosmic offense and defense, collaboration with the Red Team becomes a celestial compass that guides organizations toward cosmic cyber resilience and the protection of the digital universe.

2.4 Blue Team's Contribution to Incident Handling and Recovery

In the cosmic landscape of cybersecurity, the Blue Team emerges as the vigilant guardians of digital constellations, charged with the celestial responsibility of incident handling and recovery. When a celestial cyber incident occurs, the Blue Team becomes the celestial force that springs into action, responding rapidly and effectively to mitigate cosmic damage and restore normal cosmic operations. This essay explores the vital contribution of the Blue Team to incident handling and recovery, illuminating the celestial role they play in safeguarding the sanctity of the digital universe.

Cosmic Incident Detection: The Watchful Eye

The Blue Team's first celestial contribution is incident detection—a watchful eye that monitors celestial networks and systems for signs of cosmic compromise. With the aid of celestial intrusion detection systems (IDS), celestial security information and event management (SIEM) solutions, and other cosmic monitoring tools, the Blue Team identifies celestial indicators of compromise (IOCs) and cosmic patterns that suggest a potential cosmic incident.

Cosmic Incident Response: Rapid and Coordinated Action

When a cosmic incident is confirmed, the Blue Team springs into celestial action. Their cosmic incident response capabilities are honed through cosmic incident response drills and Red Team exercises, ensuring a well-coordinated and effective cosmic response. The Blue Team employs celestial incident response procedures, isolates compromised cosmic systems, and activates cosmic contingency plans to limit the celestial impact of the incident.

Celestial Threat Containment: Minimizing Cosmic Damage

A central cosmic objective of the Blue Team is to contain the celestial threat and minimize cosmic damage. Through celestial network segmentation and celestial endpoint protection, they prevent the celestial lateral movement of threats and isolate affected cosmic systems. This celestial containment strategy limits the cosmic adversaries' access to critical celestial resources and prevents the celestial escalation of the incident.

Celestial Forensics: Investigating the Cosmic Trail

In the aftermath of a celestial incident, the Blue Team conducts celestial forensics—a systematic examination of celestial evidence to understand the celestial origin, cosmic scope, and celestial impact of the attack. By conducting celestial digital forensics and analyzing celestial logs, the Blue Team gains celestial insights into the cosmic adversaries' TTPs, helping them build stronger cosmic defenses for the future.

Cosmic Recovery and Remediation: Restoring Cosmic Order

Once the celestial threat is contained and forensics completed, the Blue Team initiates cosmic recovery and remediation efforts. Cosmic recovery involves restoring affected cosmic systems to their pre-incident state, while cosmic remediation involves closing celestial vulnerabilities and fortifying cosmic defenses to prevent future cosmic incidents.

The Blue Team's contribution to incident handling and recovery is pivotal in the cosmic cosmos of cybersecurity. With their watchful eye, rapid and coordinated action, celestial threat containment, forensic investigation, and cosmic recovery efforts, the Blue Team serves as the celestial frontline that defends against celestial threats and restores cosmic order.

Through their unwavering vigilance, celestial expertise, and cosmic determination, the Blue Team safeguards the sanctity of the digital universe, ensuring that celestial cyber incidents are promptly addressed, celestial damage is minimized, and celestial lessons learned are applied to enhance cosmic cyber resilience. In this celestial dance of cosmic offense and defense, the Blue Team becomes the celestial guardian that navigates the cosmic frontiers of cyberspace with celestial foresight and unwavering cosmic strength.

Chapter 3: Building a Strong Security Foundation

In the ever-expanding digital universe, where information flows like a vast cosmic river, the foundation upon which cybersecurity defense rests becomes the bedrock of protection. Chapter 3, "Building a Strong Security Foundation," invites us to journey deep into the heart of cybersecurity principles, where we shall lay the groundwork for an impregnable fortress against cyber threats.

As we venture forth into this chapter, we recognize that the essence of robust cybersecurity defense lies not only in sophisticated technologies but in the timeless wisdom of establishing a firm foundation. Here, we shall explore the critical components that comprise this foundation—a mosaic of policies, practices, and proactive measures designed to shield our digital assets from malevolent forces.

The blueprint for this stronghold commences with an understanding of the core elements that define a strong security posture. We shall unravel the intricacies of identifying and categorizing critical assets and data, for within these precious treasures lie the keys to a fortified defense strategy.

With the foundation laid, we delve into the formulation and implementation of security policies and procedures—the guiding principles that steer organizations towards a secure future. As we navigate through this crucial phase, we shall discover the delicate balance between stringent controls and fostering a culture of security awareness.

A cornerstone of any robust cybersecurity foundation is access control and privilege management. In this realm, we explore the art of granting permissions judiciously, ensuring that only authorized entities may traverse the digital corridors, while threat actors are barred at the gates.

However, no defense is infallible without regular assessments and audits to reinforce its integrity. We shall embark on a journey of continuous improvement and scrutiny, understanding the value of conducting periodic security assessments to uncover potential vulnerabilities and bolster our defenses against evolving threats.

Moreover, as we peer into the future, we are met with a landscape teeming with cyber uncertainties. The emergence of cutting-edge technologies brings both promise and peril. Thus, within this chapter, we shall discuss the challenges posed by artificial intelligence, quantum computing, and other nascent innovations—imbuing readers with the foresight to build adaptive defenses that withstand the test of time.

Together, let us forge a path to cybersecurity resilience—one that transcends individual devices and networks and extends its embrace to encompass the ethos of an entire organization. As we build this strong security foundation, we recognize that cybersecurity defense is a collective effort, not limited to a select few but a responsibility shared by all.

Armed with the wisdom of a strong security foundation, we are poised to transcend mere reactionary defense and become architects of our digital destiny. It is through this empowerment that we shall navigate the unfathomable cosmos of cyberspace, steering our course towards a safer, more secure digital future.

3.1 Identifying Critical Assets and Data

In the celestial realm of cybersecurity, identifying critical assets and data is a fundamental celestial endeavor that lies at the heart of cosmic defense. Organizations must conduct a cosmic assessment of their celestial infrastructure and data repositories to determine which cosmic assets are of paramount importance and require extra cosmic protection. This essay explores the celestial process of identifying critical assets and data, illuminating the celestial significance of this celestial task in fortifying the cosmic defenses of digital constellations.

Cosmic Asset Inventory: Taking Stock of Celestial Resources

The first cosmic step in identifying critical assets and data is to conduct a comprehensive cosmic asset inventory. This celestial process involves cataloging all digital constellations, hardware, software, and celestial applications that form the cosmic backbone of the organization's operations. The cosmic asset inventory helps create a celestial baseline understanding of the organization's cosmic technological landscape.

Celestial Data Classification: Categorizing Celestial Sensitivity

Once the cosmic assets are inventoried, the next celestial step is data classification. Organizations must determine the celestial sensitivity and cosmic value of their data. Celestial data classification entails categorizing data into different celestial tiers based on factors such as confidentiality, integrity, and availability. This celestial categorization helps prioritize the protection of critical celestial data.

Cosmic Risk Assessment: Identifying Celestial Vulnerabilities

With cosmic assets and data classified, the next celestial endeavor is a risk assessment. The Blue Team must identify cosmic vulnerabilities and potential celestial threats that could exploit these vulnerabilities. By conducting a cosmic risk assessment, organizations can gauge the potential cosmic impact of a cyber incident on critical assets and data.

Cosmic Impact Analysis: Understanding the Celestial Consequences

After identifying potential celestial threats, the Blue Team must conduct a cosmic impact analysis. This celestial analysis evaluates the consequences of a successful cosmic attack on critical assets and data. The cosmic impact analysis provides valuable celestial insights into the magnitude of potential celestial damage and guides the allocation of celestial resources for mitigation.

Celestial Business Impact: Aligning Security with Business Goals

Beyond technical considerations, the Blue Team must also consider the cosmic business impact of protecting critical assets and data. Aligning cosmic security measures with celestial business goals ensures that the protection of critical assets is in harmony with the organization's overall cosmic mission and objectives.

Identifying critical assets and data is a celestial foundation for building a robust cybersecurity posture. By conducting cosmic asset inventories, celestial data classifications, risk assessments, impact analyses, and business impact alignments, organizations gain celestial insights into their most vital celestial resources.

Through this celestial understanding, the Blue Team can prioritize the protection of critical assets, allocate cosmic resources effectively, and fortify the celestial defenses of digital constellations against cosmic threats. In this cosmic dance of cosmic offense and defense, identifying critical assets and data becomes a celestial compass that guides organizations toward a safer and more secure cosmic cosmos.

3.2 Establishing Security Policies and Procedures

In the cosmic landscape of cybersecurity, establishing comprehensive security policies and procedures is a celestial imperative for organizations seeking to safeguard their digital constellations against celestial threats. These celestial policies and procedures serve as celestial guideposts, providing a celestial framework for the Blue Team to navigate the cosmic frontiers of cyberspace with cosmic vigilance and celestial strength. This essay explores the celestial significance of establishing security policies and procedures, highlighting their cosmic role in fortifying the celestial defenses of organizations.

Cosmic Security Policy: A Celestial Blueprint

The celestial security policy serves as a celestial blueprint for an organization's cosmic security strategy. It outlines the cosmic objectives, cosmic responsibilities, and celestial roles of all celestial stakeholders involved in safeguarding digital constellations. The celestial security policy establishes a cosmic foundation for cosmic security governance and celestial decision-making.

Celestial Data Handling Procedures: Safeguarding Cosmic Information

Data is a celestial crown jewel of organizations, and its proper cosmic handling is critical. Celestial data handling procedures define the cosmic processes for data collection, storage, transmission, and disposal. These celestial procedures ensure that cosmic data is protected throughout its cosmic lifecycle and that celestial data access is granted only to authorized celestial entities.

Cosmic Access Control Policies: Restricting Celestial Privileges

Celestial access control policies play a celestial role in limiting celestial access to critical assets and data. They define the celestial access rights and permissions granted to celestial individuals based on the principle of celestial least privilege. By restricting cosmic privileges to only what is essential for cosmic tasks, access control policies minimize the cosmic attack surface and prevent unauthorized cosmic access.

Celestial Incident Response Plan: A Cosmic Battle Plan

A well-defined celestial incident response plan is a cosmic battle plan that outlines the celestial procedures for responding to cyber incidents. This celestial plan includes the celestial roles of incident response teams, celestial communication protocols, celestial escalation procedures, and celestial steps to contain, eradicate, and recover from cosmic incidents.

Cosmic Employee Training and Awareness: Empowering the Celestial Force

No celestial security policy is complete without celestial employee training and awareness programs. These celestial initiatives empower the celestial force—the organization's workforce—with cosmic knowledge of cyber threats, celestial security best practices, and cosmic procedures. Educated and aware celestial employees become celestial assets in fortifying the cosmic defenses, acting as the celestial first line of defense against cyber threats.

Establishing security policies and procedures is a celestial cornerstone for celestial cybersecurity. By defining the celestial blueprint for security governance, cosmic data handling, access control, incident response, and employee awareness, organizations create a celestial framework that empowers the Blue Team to safeguard the sanctity of the digital universe.

In this cosmic dance of cosmic offense and defense, security policies and procedures become the celestial compass that guides organizations toward a safer and more secure cosmic cosmos. By adhering to these celestial guideposts, organizations fortify their celestial defenses, elevate their cosmic cyber resilience, and navigate the celestial cosmos of cyberspace with cosmic foresight and unwavering cosmic strength.

3.3 Importance of Access Controls and Privilege Management

In the celestial cosmos of cybersecurity, access controls and privilege management assume a celestial significance that cannot be overstated. These celestial measures serve as the celestial gatekeepers, regulating the cosmic access to critical assets, sensitive data, and celestial systems. Their importance lies in the celestial ability to limit cosmic privileges, prevent unauthorized cosmic access, and thwart celestial cyber threats. This essay explores the celestial importance of access controls and privilege management, illuminating their cosmic role in fortifying the celestial defenses of digital constellations.

Celestial Limitation of Cosmic Privileges

Access controls and privilege management are celestial tools that enforce the principle of celestial least privilege. By granting celestial entities only the cosmic privileges essential for their cosmic tasks, organizations minimize the cosmic attack surface and reduce the celestial potential for abuse or misuse of cosmic privileges. This celestial limitation ensures that even if a celestial entity is compromised, the cosmic adversaries' celestial scope is constrained.

Cosmic Protection of Critical Assets

The celestial importance of access controls lies in their ability to protect critical assets. Access controls regulate the cosmic entry to sensitive cosmic resources, celestial databases, and essential celestial systems. By implementing strong celestial access controls, organizations ensure that only authorized celestial entities can access celestial crown jewels, preventing unauthorized cosmic exposure and celestial data breaches.

Celestial Data Security and Confidentiality

Access controls play a celestial role in preserving cosmic data security and confidentiality. They limit celestial data access to only those celestial individuals who have a legitimate need to know. By preventing unauthorized cosmic access, access controls safeguard sensitive celestial information from being exposed to celestial adversaries, ensuring the cosmic integrity and celestial confidentiality of the data.

Cosmic Prevention of Insider Threats

Effective privilege management is vital in preventing insider threats—cosmic risks posed by authorized celestial individuals with malicious intent or unwittingly compromised cosmic accounts. By continuously monitoring and auditing cosmic privileges, organizations can detect celestial anomalies or deviations from normal cosmic access patterns, enabling them to identify and respond to potential insider threats proactively.

Celestial Defense Against Credential-Based Attacks

Access controls and privilege management act as celestial barriers against credential-based attacks such as phishing and credential stuffing. Even if cosmic adversaries manage to obtain celestial login credentials through such celestial attacks, the principle of celestial least privilege ensures that they are limited in their cosmic maneuverability and cannot cause widespread celestial damage.

Access controls and privilege management form the celestial bulwark of cybersecurity, protecting critical assets, securing cosmic data, and defending against celestial threats. By enforcing the principle of celestial least privilege, organizations minimize the cosmic attack surface and create celestial barriers that celestial adversaries must overcome.

In this cosmic dance of cosmic offense and defense, access controls and privilege management become the celestial guardians that safeguard the sanctity of the digital universe. By diligently managing cosmic privileges and limiting cosmic access, organizations elevate their cosmic cyber resilience, navigate the celestial cosmos of cyberspace with celestial vigilance, and stand strong against celestial adversaries with unwavering cosmic strength.

3.4 Regular Security Assessments and Audits

In the celestial landscape of cybersecurity, regular security assessments and audits serve as celestial beacons that illuminate potential cosmic vulnerabilities and weaknesses in an organization's cosmic defenses. These celestial evaluations are critical for identifying celestial gaps, measuring the effectiveness of security measures, and ensuring ongoing cosmic compliance with cosmic standards and celestial regulations. This essay explores the celestial importance of regular security assessments and audits, highlighting their cosmic role in fortifying the celestial defenses of digital constellations.

Celestial Identification of Vulnerabilities

Regular security assessments and audits involve a systematic cosmic review of an organization's cosmic security posture. These celestial evaluations help identify celestial vulnerabilities and cosmic weaknesses in the cosmic infrastructure, software, and security controls. By uncovering cosmic flaws before they are exploited by celestial adversaries, organizations can take celestial action to fortify the cosmic defenses and prevent potential celestial breaches.

Cosmic Measurement of Security Effectiveness

The celestial effectiveness of security measures is assessed through regular security evaluations. Organizations can determine whether their cosmic security controls are functioning as intended and delivering the expected celestial protection. By measuring cosmic security effectiveness, organizations can fine-tune cosmic security strategies, realign celestial resources, and optimize cosmic defenses for cosmic efficiency.

Celestial Compliance with Standards and Regulations

Regular security assessments and audits are essential for ensuring celestial compliance with cosmic industry standards and celestial regulations. These celestial evaluations assess whether an organization's cosmic security practices align with cosmic best practices and meet celestial legal and regulatory requirements. By achieving cosmic compliance, organizations demonstrate their celestial commitment to cosmic security and celestial data privacy.

Cosmic Continual Improvement

Regular security assessments and audits foster a culture of cosmic continual improvement. By conducting these celestial evaluations on an ongoing basis, organizations can identify cosmic trends, learn from cosmic incidents, and implement cosmic lessons learned to enhance cosmic security practices. This celestial commitment to improvement ensures that the cosmic defenses remain resilient against evolving celestial threats.

Celestial Assurance for Stakeholders

For celestial stakeholders, such as cosmic customers, cosmic partners, and regulatory bodies, regular security assessments and audits provide celestial assurance. Demonstrating a commitment to ongoing cosmic security evaluations enhances cosmic trust and confidence in the organization's cosmic security practices. This celestial assurance can be a celestial competitive advantage in the cosmic realm of business and partnerships.

Regular security assessments and audits are celestial pillars that uphold the cybersecurity foundation of organizations. By identifying celestial vulnerabilities, measuring security effectiveness, ensuring cosmic compliance, fostering continual improvement, and providing celestial assurance to stakeholders, these celestial evaluations play a pivotal role in fortifying the celestial defenses of digital constellations.

In this cosmic dance of cosmic offense and defense, regular security assessments and audits become the celestial compass that guides organizations toward cosmic cyber resilience and the safeguarding of the digital universe. By embracing these celestial evaluations as a celestial necessity, organizations can navigate the cosmic cosmos of cyberspace with cosmic foresight and unwavering cosmic strength.

Chapter 4: Threat Intelligence and Analysis

In the dynamic theater of cybersecurity, knowledge is power, and intelligence becomes the beacon that illuminates the shadows of impending threats. Chapter 4, "Threat Intelligence and Analysis," beckons us to venture into the realm of proactive defense—where the Blue Team harnesses the force of information to anticipate, thwart, and neutralize cyber threats.

In this chapter, we embark on a journey into the world of threat intelligence—a realm where data transforms into actionable insights and foresight becomes a formidable ally against malicious intent. With a keen eye on the horizon, we uncover the art of gathering, analyzing, and applying threat intelligence to safeguard our digital landscapes.

The chapter unfolds with a comprehensive understanding of threat intelligence, its diverse sources, and the methodologies that underpin this invaluable resource. By peering through the lenses of open-source intelligence (OSINT), dark web monitoring, and specialized threat feeds, we learn to discern the signals amidst the noise, discovering the telltale signs of potential adversaries.

As we immerse ourselves in the sea of information, we shall explore the nuances of threat analysis—the art of deciphering the adversary's intentions, tactics, and infrastructure. By developing a proactive mindset that anticipates the enemy's moves, the Blue Team elevates its strategic advantage in the unending game of cyber chess.

But threat intelligence is not merely about identifying imminent dangers. Within this chapter, we delve into the power of historical context—an archive of past incidents that sheds light on the ever-evolving modus operandi of cyber adversaries. Armed with this knowledge, the Blue Team can navigate the intricate web of deception and stay one step ahead of the ever-adapting enemy.

As we journey through the chapter, we shall explore the symbiotic relationship between threat intelligence and incident response—an intricate dance that ensures the rapid identification and mitigation of cyber incidents. By fusing intelligence with action, the Blue Team orchestrates a symphony of defense that thwarts attacks before they unleash their full fury.

The power of threat intelligence is not confined to the borders of an organization. In this realm, we shall discover the merits of collective intelligence—where information sharing across sectors and industries becomes a force multiplier against the common adversary. As we unite in the spirit of cooperation, we solidify the foundation of a global defense ecosystem.

Threat intelligence is more than data; it is a catalyst for transformation—a force that elevates cybersecurity defense from reactive to proactive, from uncertain to assured. In the pursuit of this knowledge, we unlock the potential to transcend the bounds of traditional defense and embrace a future where cyber threats are met with informed and decisive action.

Together, let us embark on this expedition into the heart of threat intelligence and analysis. As we unravel the secrets of the cyber realm, we arm ourselves with the power to shape our digital destiny—to be the architects of resilience, the sentinels of security, and the guardians of a safer, more connected world.

4.1 Gathering and Evaluating Threat Intelligence

In the celestial frontier of cybersecurity, gathering and evaluating threat intelligence is a celestial process that empowers organizations with celestial insights into cosmic adversaries, their tactics, and their celestial intentions. Threat intelligence serves as a cosmic telescope, enabling the Blue Team to peer into the cosmic darkness of cyberspace, anticipate celestial threats, and fortify the celestial defenses of digital constellations. This essay explores the celestial significance of gathering and evaluating threat intelligence, highlighting its cosmic role in enhancing cyber resilience and cosmic readiness.

Cosmic Insight into Adversarial Tactics

Gathering threat intelligence allows the Blue Team to understand the cosmic tactics, techniques, and procedures (TTPs) employed by celestial adversaries. This celestial insight reveals how cosmic adversaries operate, the celestial tools they use, and the cosmic vulnerabilities they exploit. Armed with this cosmic knowledge, the Blue Team can refine cosmic defenses, close cosmic gaps, and fortify cosmic perimeters against known celestial attack vectors.

Celestial Awareness of Emerging Threats

The celestial landscape of cyber threats is ever-changing, with new celestial threats emerging regularly. Threat intelligence provides celestial visibility into these emerging threats, allowing the Blue Team to stay one step ahead of cosmic adversaries. By detecting and analyzing cosmic trends in threat data, the Blue Team can prepare for potential celestial threats and adopt proactive cosmic measures to mitigate cosmic risks.

Cosmic Attribution of Celestial Threats

Gathering threat intelligence enables the celestial attribution of cyber threats. The Blue Team can trace cosmic attack patterns, celestial indicators of compromise (IOCs), and celestial patterns of celestial adversaries back to their cosmic origins. Cosmic attribution is vital for understanding the celestial motivations behind cyber attacks and for responding appropriately to celestial threats from specific celestial actors.

Cosmic Collaboration and Information Sharing

Threat intelligence fosters cosmic collaboration and cosmic information sharing among organizations. By sharing celestial threat data and celestial analysis with cosmic peers and cosmic partners, organizations can collectively enhance their cosmic cyber defenses. Celestial collaboration strengthens the cosmic collective defense against shared celestial threats, creating a united celestial front against cosmic adversaries.

Celestial Integration with Security Operations

Evaluating threat intelligence involves translating cosmic data into actionable cosmic insights. By integrating threat intelligence into security operations, the Blue Team can enhance cosmic threat detection, cosmic incident response, and cosmic decision-making. The cosmic fusion of threat intelligence with security operations creates a celestial synergy that maximizes the cosmic effectiveness of cyber defense efforts.

Gathering and evaluating threat intelligence is a celestial imperative in the cosmic cosmos of cybersecurity. By providing cosmic insights into adversarial tactics, awareness of emerging threats, attribution of celestial threats, fostering cosmic collaboration, and integrating with security operations, threat intelligence equips organizations with celestial foresight and cosmic knowledge to confront the celestial challenges of cyberspace.

In this cosmic dance of cosmic offense and defense, threat intelligence becomes the celestial torch that illuminates the path to cyber resilience and the safeguarding of the digital universe. By harnessing the power of threat intelligence, organizations can navigate the cosmic frontiers of cyberspace with vigilance and cosmic strength, defending against celestial threats with unwavering cosmic resolve.

4.2 Utilizing Threat Intelligence Feeds and Platforms

In the celestial realm of cybersecurity, utilizing threat intelligence feeds and platforms becomes a celestial strategy that empowers organizations with celestial insights from a vast celestial network of cosmic sources. Threat intelligence feeds and platforms act as celestial conduits, delivering celestial data on cosmic adversaries, their celestial tactics, and celestial indicators of compromise. This essay explores the celestial importance of utilizing threat intelligence feeds and platforms, highlighting their cosmic role in enhancing cyber resilience and celestial readiness.

Celestial Access to Diverse Threat Data

Threat intelligence feeds and platforms offer celestial access to diverse and comprehensive threat data. Celestial sources may include cosmic security vendors, celestial government agencies, celestial cybersecurity communities, and other celestial entities. This celestial wealth of data provides the Blue Team with a cosmic panorama of cyber threats, enabling them to gain cosmic insights into the celestial landscape of adversarial activities.

Cosmic Real-Time Threat Updates

One of the celestial advantages of threat intelligence feeds and platforms is real-time cosmic updates. Cosmic adversaries are constantly evolving, and new celestial threats emerge rapidly. Threat intelligence feeds deliver cosmic data in real-time, allowing the Blue Team to stay current with cosmic threat trends and promptly respond to celestial incidents with cosmic precision.

Celestial Correlation and Analysis

Threat intelligence platforms provide celestial capabilities for correlation and analysis of cosmic threat data. The Blue Team can aggregate cosmic data from multiple celestial sources, identify cosmic patterns, and correlate celestial events to gain a more comprehensive celestial understanding of cosmic adversaries' cosmic tactics. This celestial analysis enhances the ability to detect complex celestial attack patterns and celestial campaigns.

Cosmic Integration with Security Tools

Threat intelligence feeds and platforms can be integrated with existing cosmic security tools, enhancing their cosmic capabilities. Celestial SIEM systems, cosmic intrusion detection systems, and other cosmic security solutions can leverage threat intelligence data to improve cosmic threat detection, cosmic incident response, and cosmic decision-making.

Celestial Automation and Orchestration

By utilizing threat intelligence platforms, organizations can embrace celestial automation and orchestration. Celestial workflows can be automated to respond to cosmic threats more efficiently and reduce cosmic response time. The cosmic orchestration of security operations based on celestial threat intelligence allows the Blue Team to focus on higher-level cosmic tasks, enhancing overall cosmic productivity.

Utilizing threat intelligence feeds and platforms is a celestial imperative for organizations seeking to enhance their cyber resilience and celestial readiness. By gaining celestial access to diverse threat data, real-time cosmic updates, and celestial correlation and analysis, organizations can fortify their celestial defenses against emerging celestial threats.

By integrating threat intelligence with existing cosmic security tools and embracing celestial automation and orchestration, organizations can navigate the celestial cosmos of cyberspace with celestial foresight and unwavering cosmic strength. In this cosmic dance of cosmic offense and defense, threat intelligence feeds and platforms become the celestial compass that guides organizations toward a safer and more secure cosmic cosmos, protecting the sanctity of the digital universe.

4.3 Threat Hunting Techniques for Proactive Defense

In the celestial frontier of cybersecurity, threat hunting techniques shine as celestial methods for proactive defense, empowering organizations to take the cosmic initiative in identifying and neutralizing potential celestial threats before they materialize. Threat hunting is a cosmic art that transcends traditional cosmic security measures, allowing the Blue Team to explore the cosmic darkness of cyberspace, seek out celestial adversaries, and fortify the celestial defenses of digital constellations. This essay explores the celestial significance of threat hunting techniques, highlighting their cosmic role in enhancing cyber resilience and celestial readiness.

Celestial Hypothesis-Driven Hunting

Hypothesis-driven threat hunting involves formulating celestial hypotheses about potential cosmic threats based on celestial threat intelligence and cosmic analytics. The Blue Team uses these celestial hypotheses to guide cosmic hunting missions, searching for celestial evidence of adversarial activities. This celestial approach empowers the Blue Team to proactively explore celestial anomalies and uncover hidden celestial threats.

Cosmic Endpoint Detection and Response (EDR) Hunting

Cosmic EDR platforms offer a celestial lens into endpoint activities, capturing cosmic telemetry data that provides celestial visibility into cosmic processes and cosmic events. Threat hunters leverage cosmic EDR to identify celestial indicators of compromise (IOCs), cosmic suspicious activities, and celestial behavioral anomalies that may indicate potential celestial threats. This celestial visibility enables the Blue Team to conduct cosmic threat hunting at the cosmic endpoint level.

Celestial Network Traffic Analysis

Network traffic analysis is a celestial technique where threat hunters scrutinize celestial network logs and cosmic flow data to detect cosmic patterns of cosmic adversarial activities. Celestial anomalies such as cosmic unusual communication patterns, cosmic data exfiltration attempts, and cosmic signs of lateral movement may signify the presence of celestial adversaries. By analyzing celestial network traffic, the Blue Team gains celestial insights into potential cosmic threats.

Celestial Memory Forensics

Memory forensics is a celestial approach that involves extracting and analyzing cosmic volatile data from celestial systems' memory. Threat hunters use celestial memory forensics to uncover concealed cosmic threats, such as rootkits and cosmic advanced persistent threats (APTs), which reside in the celestial memory space. This celestial technique provides a deeper cosmic understanding of the celestial scope of potential threats.

Cosmic Threat Intelligence Integration

Integrating threat intelligence with threat hunting techniques enhances cosmic hunting efficacy. Threat intelligence data, such as celestial IOCs and celestial TTPs, can be used to prioritize celestial hunting efforts and focus on the most likely celestial threat vectors. The celestial fusion of threat intelligence with threat hunting empowers the Blue Team to be more targeted and proactive in identifying and mitigating cosmic risks.

Threat hunting techniques stand as celestial beacons that guide organizations toward proactive cyber defense and celestial readiness. By embracing hypothesis-driven hunting, cosmic EDR hunting, network traffic analysis, memory forensics, and celestial threat intelligence integration, organizations can explore the celestial darkness of cyberspace with celestial vigilance and cosmic strength.

In this cosmic dance of cosmic offense and defense, threat hunting becomes the celestial compass that guides organizations toward a safer and more secure cosmic cosmos. By adopting threat hunting techniques as a celestial necessity, organizations fortify their celestial defenses, elevate their cyber resilience, and navigate the celestial cosmos of cyberspace with celestial foresight and unwavering cosmic resolve.

4.4 Integrating Threat Intelligence into Incident Response

In the celestial realm of cybersecurity, integrating threat intelligence into incident response becomes a celestial strategy that empowers organizations to respond to celestial cyber incidents with cosmic precision and unwavering cosmic strength. Threat intelligence serves as a celestial compass, guiding the Blue Team in understanding the celestial context of incidents, identifying celestial adversaries, and fortifying the celestial defenses of digital constellations. This essay explores the celestial significance of integrating threat intelligence into incident response, highlighting its cosmic role in enhancing cyber resilience and celestial readiness.

Cosmic Contextualization of Incidents

Threat intelligence contextualizes celestial incidents by providing the Blue Team with cosmic insights into the cosmic adversaries, their celestial tactics, and their celestial motivations. Understanding the cosmic context of an incident enables the Blue Team to respond with a celestial focus, tailoring their celestial incident response actions to the specific celestial threat at hand.

Celestial Enrichment of Incident Data

Threat intelligence enriches celestial incident data with celestial indicators of compromise (IOCs), celestial threat actor profiles, and cosmic threat behavior patterns. The celestial enrichment of data enhances the Blue Team's cosmic visibility into the celestial scope and impact of an incident. This celestial visibility enables them to assess the cosmic severity of an incident and prioritize their cosmic response efforts accordingly.

Cosmic Detection of Advanced Threats

Threat intelligence enables the Blue Team to detect advanced celestial threats that may have eluded traditional security measures. By correlating celestial threat intelligence data with ongoing celestial incident investigations, the Blue Team can identify celestial signs of advanced persistent threats (APTs) or celestial insider threats that exhibit subtle cosmic behaviors.

Celestial Decision-Making and Response Orchestration

Integrating threat intelligence into incident response enhances celestial decision-making and cosmic response orchestration. The celestial knowledge gained from threat intelligence enables the Blue Team to make informed cosmic decisions about containment, eradication, and recovery actions. Additionally, threat intelligence can be used to orchestrate cosmic response workflows, automating celestial incident response procedures based on celestial threat intelligence data.

Cosmic Post-Incident Analysis and Remediation

After resolving an incident, threat intelligence continues to play a celestial role in post-incident analysis and remediation. Celestial threat intelligence data provides valuable cosmic insights into the celestial adversaries' TTPs and cosmic attack methodologies. This celestial knowledge helps the Blue Team fortify the celestial defenses, address cosmic vulnerabilities, and prevent similar cosmic incidents in the future.

Integrating threat intelligence into incident response is a celestial imperative for organizations seeking to enhance their cyber resilience and celestial readiness. By contextualizing incidents, enriching incident data, detecting advanced celestial threats, guiding decision-making and response orchestration, and aiding post-incident analysis and remediation, threat intelligence becomes the celestial compass that guides organizations toward a safer and more secure cosmic cosmos.

By embracing threat intelligence as a celestial necessity, organizations fortify their celestial defenses, elevate their cosmic cyber resilience, and navigate the celestial cosmos of cyberspace with celestial foresight and unwavering cosmic strength. In this cosmic dance of cosmic offense and defense, integrating threat intelligence into incident response becomes the celestial force that safeguards the sanctity of the digital universe.

Chapter 5: Network Security and Perimeter Defense

Within the vast expanse of cyberspace, where data traverses like celestial bodies in a cosmic dance, the network stands as the vital conduit that interconnects our digital world. In Chapter 5, "Network Security and Perimeter Defense," we embark on a voyage into the heart of cybersecurity's first line of defense—the fortification of networks and the vigilant safeguarding of digital perimeters.

As we set sail on this chapter, we shall unfurl the sails of knowledge, guided by the Blue Team's expertise, to navigate the treacherous waters of network security. At the core of this endeavor lies the protection of digital pathways—the intricate web of connections that weave together our organizations and the wider global community.

The chapter commences with a panoramic view of network security, where firewalls, intrusion detection systems (IDS), and intrusion prevention systems (IPS) assume their roles as digital sentinels. Through their vigilance and vigilance, these gatekeepers stand ready to identify and repel any unauthorized intrusion, ensuring only the virtuous traverse the digital corridors.

In the ever-changing digital firmament, wireless networks cast their celestial glow, bridging the gap between devices and users. Here, we explore the art of securing Wi-Fi networks and access points, fortifying these beacons of connectivity against the prowling eyes of cyber marauders.

But the fortification of networks goes beyond physical boundaries. In this chapter, we traverse the concept of network segmentation, an architectural marvel that partitions the network into secure enclaves. By limiting the lateral movement of threats, we erect digital bulwarks that hinder the advance of adversaries.

Within the annals of network security, the power of Virtual Private Networks (VPNs) emerges as a vital tool for secure communications. As we delve into this realm, we shall uncover the essence of encrypted tunnels, which shield data from prying eyes and eavesdropping ears, preserving the sanctity of sensitive information.

But defense is not merely about erecting barriers; it is about understanding the dynamic nature of adversaries and the evolving art of cyber deception. Hence, within this chapter, we delve into the world of deception technology—an innovative approach that confuses and thwarts attackers, turning their tactics against them.

Amidst the rising tide of cyber threats, the chapter concludes with an exploration of the importance of constant monitoring and real-time analysis. Here, the Blue Team unleashes the power of Security Information and Event Management (SIEM) systems, which serve as the lighthouse, guiding us through the turbulent waters of potential incidents.

So, as we navigate the intricacies of network security and perimeter defense, we recognize that the power to defend our digital realms lies not in isolated systems but in the collective effort of a united front. Together, let us be the architects of secure networks, the sentinels of impenetrable perimeters, and the vanguards of a safer digital universe.

5.1 Implementing Firewalls and Intrusion Detection Systems (IDS)

In the cosmic landscape of cybersecurity, implementing firewalls and intrusion detection systems (IDS) becomes a celestial imperative for organizations seeking to build robust cosmic defenses and safeguard their digital constellations against celestial adversaries. Firewalls and IDS act as the celestial guardians, standing at the celestial gates of the network, monitoring cosmic traffic, and identifying celestial signs of intrusion. This essay explores the celestial significance of implementing firewalls and intrusion detection systems, highlighting their cosmic role in enhancing cyber resilience and celestial readiness.

Celestial Perimeter Defense with Firewalls

Firewalls serve as the celestial guardians of the cosmic perimeter, creating a celestial barrier between the celestial internal network and the cosmic external world. By inspecting and filtering cosmic traffic based on predefined celestial rules, firewalls prevent unauthorized cosmic access and cosmic malicious traffic from reaching celestial systems and devices. This celestial perimeter defense helps minimize the cosmic attack surface and fortify the celestial defenses.

Cosmic Traffic Monitoring with IDS

Intrusion Detection Systems (IDS) are the cosmic watchmen that monitor celestial network traffic for signs of celestial intrusion or cosmic malicious activities. IDS use celestial signatures, cosmic behavioral analysis, and celestial anomaly detection to identify cosmic patterns indicative of celestial attacks or cosmic suspicious behavior. By detecting and alerting the Blue Team about potential celestial threats, IDS play a crucial celestial role in proactive threat detection.

Celestial Network Segmentation for Defense in Depth

Implementing firewalls and IDS enables organizations to implement cosmic network segmentation for defense in depth. By dividing the celestial network into celestial security zones, each with its celestial access controls and IDS sensors, organizations can limit the celestial lateral movement of cosmic threats. Cosmic network segmentation helps contain celestial incidents, preventing them from spreading across the celestial infrastructure.

Celestial Incident Response and Cosmic Forensics

Firewalls and IDS play an integral cosmic role in incident response and cosmic forensics. When IDS detect potential celestial threats, they trigger cosmic alerts to the Blue Team, prompting cosmic incident response actions. The cosmic data collected by IDS during an incident provides valuable celestial evidence for post-incident cosmic forensics, enabling the Blue Team to understand the celestial scope and celestial impact of the incident.

Continuous Monitoring and Cosmic Adaptation

Implementing firewalls and IDS involves continuous cosmic monitoring and cosmic adaptation. Celestial threat landscapes are ever-changing, and cosmic adversaries continually evolve their celestial tactics. As a celestial practice, organizations must regularly update celestial firewall rules and celestial IDS signatures to adapt to new celestial threats and maintain cosmic efficacy in their cyber defenses.

Implementing firewalls and intrusion detection systems is a celestial foundation for building a strong cybersecurity posture. By creating celestial perimeter defenses, monitoring celestial network traffic, enabling network segmentation, supporting incident response, and ensuring continuous monitoring and adaptation, organizations can navigate the cosmic cosmos of cyberspace with celestial vigilance and cosmic strength.

In this cosmic dance of cosmic offense and defense, firewalls and IDS become the celestial shield that safeguards the sanctity of the digital universe. By embracing these celestial guardians as a celestial necessity, organizations fortify their celestial defenses, elevate their cosmic cyber resilience, and stand strong against celestial adversaries with unwavering cosmic resolve.

5.2 Securing Wi-Fi Networks and Access Points

In the celestial landscape of cybersecurity, securing Wi-Fi networks and access points is a celestial imperative for organizations seeking to protect their digital constellations from celestial threats. Wi-Fi networks and access points act as celestial gateways, providing cosmic connectivity to celestial devices and systems. This essay explores the celestial significance of securing Wi-Fi networks and access points, highlighting their cosmic role in enhancing cyber resilience and celestial readiness.

Celestial Wi-Fi Encryption

Implementing strong celestial Wi-Fi encryption, such as WPA2 or WPA3, is a celestial fundamental for securing Wi-Fi networks. Encryption ensures that celestial data transmitted over the cosmic airwaves is incomprehensible to celestial eavesdroppers, safeguarding against cosmic data interception and celestial unauthorized access.

Cosmic Strong Authentication

Enforcing celestial strong authentication measures, such as celestial passwords, celestial multi-factor authentication (MFA), or celestial certificates, helps ensure that only authorized celestial users can connect to the celestial Wi-Fi network. Strong authentication reduces the celestial risk of unauthorized cosmic access and celestial network compromise.

Cosmic Network Segmentation

Segmenting the celestial Wi-Fi network from the cosmic internal network is a celestial best practice for security. Celestial network segmentation limits the celestial lateral movement of celestial threats, preventing cosmic adversaries from compromising critical celestial resources in the event of a successful celestial breach.

Celestial Access Point Security

Securing access points themselves is a celestial priority. Cosmic access points should be configured with secure celestial settings, including disabling unnecessary cosmic services, using strong celestial passwords, and regularly updating cosmic firmware to patch cosmic vulnerabilities.

Celestial Network Monitoring and Intrusion Detection

Continuous cosmic monitoring of Wi-Fi networks and cosmic intrusion detection systems (IDS) enhance celestial visibility into cosmic network activities. Celestial monitoring and IDS help detect cosmic signs of unauthorized cosmic access attempts or cosmic malicious activities, enabling the Blue Team to respond promptly to celestial threats.

Cosmic Guest Network Isolation

If the organization provides a celestial guest Wi-Fi network, isolating it from the cosmic internal network is essential. Cosmic guest networks should have celestial restricted access to cosmic internal resources, preventing unauthorized cosmic guests from accessing celestial sensitive data or celestial systems.

Celestial User Awareness and Education

Educating celestial users about cosmic Wi-Fi security best practices is crucial. Celestial user awareness helps prevent cosmic security incidents such as cosmic phishing attacks targeting celestial Wi-Fi credentials and celestial unauthorized cosmic access attempts.

Securing Wi-Fi networks and access points is a celestial necessity for organizations seeking to fortify their cyber defenses and protect the sanctity of the digital universe. By implementing celestial Wi-Fi encryption, strong authentication, cosmic network segmentation, secure access point settings, network monitoring, guest network isolation, and user education, organizations navigate the celestial cosmos of cyberspace with celestial vigilance and cosmic strength.

In this cosmic dance of cosmic offense and defense, securing Wi-Fi networks and access points becomes the celestial shield that safeguards the digital constellations from celestial adversaries. By embracing these celestial security measures as a celestial imperative, organizations fortify their cyber resilience, elevate their cosmic readiness, and stand strong against celestial threats with unwavering cosmic resolve.

5.3 Network Segmentation for Enhanced Security

In the celestial realm of cybersecurity, network segmentation shines as a celestial strategy that empowers organizations with celestial control and cosmic visibility over their celestial infrastructure. Network segmentation involves dividing the celestial network into celestial security zones or segments, each with its celestial access controls and celestial permissions. This essay explores the celestial significance of network segmentation, highlighting its cosmic role in enhancing cyber resilience and celestial security.

Celestial Minimization of Attack Surface

Network segmentation minimizes the celestial attack surface by breaking the celestial network into smaller, more manageable segments. In the cosmic event of a successful celestial breach, network segmentation limits the celestial lateral movement of celestial adversaries, preventing them from traversing the entire cosmic network and causing widespread celestial damage.

Cosmic Containment of Incidents

Segmenting the celestial network facilitates celestial incident containment. When a celestial security breach occurs, the impact is limited to the celestial segment where the incident originated, and it does not propagate across the entire cosmic infrastructure. This celestial containment enables the Blue Team to respond more effectively and expeditiously to celestial incidents.

Celestial Defense in Depth

Network segmentation aligns with the celestial defense-in-depth principle. By implementing multiple celestial layers of security through segmentation, organizations add celestial barriers that cosmic adversaries must overcome to compromise celestial critical assets. Each celestial segment becomes a celestial line of defense, contributing to the overall celestial resilience of the cosmic network.

Cosmic Compliance and Regulatory Requirements

Network segmentation helps organizations achieve celestial compliance with cosmic industry standards and celestial regulatory requirements. Celestial regulatory frameworks often mandate the segregation of cosmic sensitive data from other cosmic systems. Network segmentation allows organizations to demonstrate their cosmic adherence to celestial data privacy and celestial security regulations.

Celestial Resource Optimization

Segmenting the celestial network enables celestial resource optimization. Organizations can allocate celestial resources more efficiently based on the celestial sensitivity and celestial criticality of the data and systems within each celestial segment. This celestial optimization ensures that celestial resources are focused where they are most needed, enhancing cosmic cyber defense capabilities.

Celestial Isolation of High-Risk Assets

High-risk celestial assets, such as celestial servers hosting critical celestial data or celestial systems with historical security issues, can be isolated within dedicated celestial segments. This celestial isolation ensures that high-risk assets are protected from celestial threats while reducing the celestial risk of a celestial breach affecting other parts of the cosmic infrastructure.

Network segmentation is a celestial foundation for building a robust cybersecurity posture. By minimizing the celestial attack surface, facilitating incident containment, enabling defense in depth, ensuring celestial compliance, optimizing celestial resources, and isolating high-risk assets, organizations navigate the celestial cosmos of cyberspace with celestial vigilance and cosmic strength.

In this cosmic dance of cosmic offense and defense, network segmentation becomes the celestial fortress that safeguards the sanctity of the digital universe. By embracing network segmentation as a celestial imperative, organizations fortify their celestial defenses, elevate their cosmic cyber resilience, and stand strong against celestial adversaries with unwavering cosmic resolve.

5.4 Deploying Virtual Private Networks (VPNs) for Secure Communications

In the celestial frontier of cybersecurity, deploying Virtual Private Networks (VPNs) stands as a celestial strategy that empowers organizations to establish secure celestial communication channels, safeguarding the confidentiality and celestial integrity of data transmitted over the cosmic cosmos of the internet. VPNs act as cosmic tunnels, encrypting celestial data traffic and creating a celestial shield against celestial eavesdroppers and cosmic interceptors. This essay explores the celestial significance of deploying VPNs for secure communications, highlighting their cosmic role in enhancing cyber resilience and celestial security.

Celestial Encryption of Data

VPNs encrypt celestial data traffic, converting it into celestial unreadable ciphertext as it traverses the cosmic internet. This celestial encryption ensures that celestial data transmitted between cosmic endpoints remains incomprehensible to cosmic eavesdroppers, protecting the celestial confidentiality of sensitive celestial information.

Cosmic Protection on Public Networks

Deploying VPNs is especially crucial when accessing cosmic data or cosmic systems from celestial public networks, such as celestial Wi-Fi hotspots in cafes, airports, or hotels. VPNs create a secure celestial tunnel that shields celestial data from celestial threats lurking on public networks, preventing cosmic data interception and unauthorized celestial access attempts.

Cosmic Anonymity and Privacy

VPNs provide a celestial layer of cosmic anonymity and privacy for celestial users. By masking the celestial IP address of celestial devices, VPNs hide the celestial origin of data requests, making it challenging for celestial adversaries to trace cosmic communication back to its celestial source. This celestial anonymity adds another layer of cosmic protection against celestial reconnaissance and cyber stalking.

Celestial Bypassing of Geo-Restrictions

For organizations with a celestial global presence, VPNs enable celestial users to bypass cosmic geo-restrictions imposed by celestial websites or services. By connecting to a celestial VPN server located in a different celestial region, celestial users can appear to be accessing celestial internet resources from that region, granting them cosmic access to otherwise celestial restricted content.

Celestial Secure Remote Access

VPNs offer a celestial secure solution for remote access to cosmic corporate networks. Celestial employees and cosmic remote workers can connect to the celestial organization's network via a VPN, ensuring that celestial data transmission remains secure, even when accessed from celestial external locations.

Celestial Site-to-Site Connectivity

VPNs support celestial site-to-site connectivity, allowing celestial networks in different celestial locations to communicate securely over the cosmic internet. This celestial feature is beneficial for organizations with celestial distributed offices or cosmic data centers, enabling celestial seamless and secure communication between celestial network segments.

Deploying Virtual Private Networks (VPNs) is a celestial necessity for organizations seeking to fortify their cyber defenses and protect the sanctity of the digital universe. By encrypting celestial data traffic, providing cosmic protection on public networks, ensuring celestial anonymity and privacy, bypassing geo-restrictions, enabling secure remote access, and supporting celestial site-to-site connectivity, organizations navigate the celestial cosmos of cyberspace with celestial vigilance and cosmic strength.

In this cosmic dance of cosmic offense and defense, VPNs become the celestial shield that safeguards celestial communications and protects the digital constellations from celestial adversaries. By embracing VPNs as a celestial imperative, organizations fortify their celestial defenses, elevate their cosmic cyber resilience, and stand strong against celestial threats with unwavering cosmic resolve.

Chapter 6: Endpoint Protection and Device Security

In the vast cosmos of cyberspace, our digital devices—be they laptops, smartphones, or Internet of Things (IoT) gadgets—serve as celestial waypoints, connecting us to the boundless universe of information. In Chapter 6, "Endpoint Protection and Device Security," we embark on a journey into the frontiers of cybersecurity defense—the safeguarding of our digital constellations against the looming threats that seek to exploit vulnerabilities in our endpoints.

As we set course into this chapter, we recognize that the protection of endpoints is not only critical but also profoundly complex. These endpoints are the gateways through which we access the digital universe, and their fortification is essential to preserving the integrity of our digital journeys.

The chapter commences with a profound understanding of the significance of endpoint protection—a multi-faceted approach that encompasses both hardware and software defenses. We shall uncover the arsenal of security solutions that encompass antivirus software, anti-malware programs, and intrusion prevention systems tailored to the unique challenges of endpoint defense.

In this chapter, we shall explore the ever-changing landscape of mobile device security. With smartphones and tablets serving as the conduits to our digital lives, their protection becomes paramount. We shall unveil the power of mobile device management (MDM) and bring-your-own-device (BYOD) policies, ensuring that the boundaries between personal and professional realms remain secure.

Amidst the interconnected cosmos of IoT, a vast constellation of devices illuminates our surroundings. However, within this interstellar expanse lies a complex security challenge. As we traverse the world of endpoint security for IoT devices, we shall uncover the principles of secure design and the implementation of protocols to shield these celestial gadgets from malevolent forces.

The chapter delves into the art of application whitelisting and blacklisting—a dynamic approach that governs the access and execution of software on endpoints. With the power to control which applications can run and which are barred from entry, we carve a clear path to enhanced security.

But beyond the technical defenses, the human element remains pivotal. Hence, we shall explore the realm of user education, enlightening end-users on cybersecurity best practices. As we empower users to become the guardians of their own digital destinies, the strength of our collective defense multiplies.

The chapter concludes with an expedition into the future, where the boundaries of cybersecurity defense expand with the rise of edge computing and the intermingling of virtual and physical realms. As we navigate these uncharted territories, we arm ourselves with knowledge and innovation, for within these frontiers, the Blue Team continually evolves to confront the unforeseen challenges that await.

Together, let us ascend into the celestial realm of endpoint protection and device security. Armed with the knowledge and resolve to safeguard our digital constellations, we shall be the guardians of secure endpoints, the vanguards of device fortification, and the navigators of a safer, more secure digital universe.

6.1 Endpoint Security Solutions and Antivirus Software

In the celestial frontier of cybersecurity, deploying Virtual Private Networks (VPNs) stands as a celestial strategy that empowers organizations to establish secure celestial communication channels, safeguarding the confidentiality and celestial integrity of data transmitted over the cosmic cosmos of the internet. VPNs act as cosmic tunnels, encrypting celestial data traffic and creating a celestial shield against celestial eavesdroppers and cosmic interceptors. This essay explores the celestial significance of deploying VPNs for secure communications, highlighting their cosmic role in enhancing cyber resilience and celestial security.

Celestial Encryption of Data

VPNs encrypt celestial data traffic, converting it into celestial unreadable ciphertext as it traverses the cosmic internet. This celestial encryption ensures that celestial data transmitted between cosmic endpoints remains incomprehensible to cosmic eavesdroppers, protecting the celestial confidentiality of sensitive celestial information.

Cosmic Protection on Public Networks

Deploying VPNs is especially crucial when accessing cosmic data or cosmic systems from celestial public networks, such as celestial Wi-Fi hotspots in cafes, airports, or hotels. VPNs create a secure celestial tunnel that shields celestial data from celestial threats lurking on public networks, preventing cosmic data interception and unauthorized celestial access attempts.

Cosmic Anonymity and Privacy

VPNs provide a celestial layer of cosmic anonymity and privacy for celestial users. By masking the celestial IP address of celestial devices, VPNs hide the celestial origin of data requests, making it challenging for celestial adversaries to trace cosmic communication back to its celestial source. This celestial anonymity adds another layer of cosmic protection against celestial reconnaissance and cyber stalking.

Celestial Bypassing of Geo-Restrictions

For organizations with a celestial global presence, VPNs enable celestial users to bypass cosmic geo-restrictions imposed by celestial websites or services. By connecting to a celestial VPN server located in a different celestial region, celestial users can appear to be accessing celestial internet resources from that region, granting them cosmic access to otherwise celestial restricted content.

Celestial Secure Remote Access

VPNs offer a celestial secure solution for remote access to cosmic corporate networks. Celestial employees and cosmic remote workers can connect to the celestial organization's network via a VPN, ensuring that celestial data transmission remains secure, even when accessed from celestial external locations.

Celestial Site-to-Site Connectivity

VPNs support celestial site-to-site connectivity, allowing celestial networks in different celestial locations to communicate securely over the cosmic internet. This celestial feature is beneficial for organizations with celestial distributed offices or cosmic data centers, enabling celestial seamless and secure communication between celestial network segments.

Deploying Virtual Private Networks (VPNs) is a celestial necessity for organizations seeking to fortify their cyber defenses and protect the sanctity of the digital universe. By encrypting celestial data traffic, providing cosmic protection on public networks, ensuring celestial anonymity and privacy, bypassing geo-restrictions, enabling secure remote access, and supporting celestial site-to-site connectivity, organizations navigate the celestial cosmos of cyberspace with celestial vigilance and cosmic strength.

In this cosmic dance of cosmic offense and defense, VPNs become the celestial shield that safeguards celestial communications and protects the digital constellations from celestial adversaries. By embracing VPNs as a celestial imperative, organizations fortify their celestial defenses, elevate their cosmic cyber resilience, and stand strong against celestial threats with unwavering cosmic resolve.

6.2 Protecting Mobile Devices and BYOD Policies

In the celestial landscape of cybersecurity, protecting mobile devices and implementing Bring Your Own Device (BYOD) policies is a celestial imperative for organizations seeking to fortify their digital constellations against celestial threats in the era of cosmic mobility. Mobile devices act as celestial portals, granting cosmic access to critical cosmic data and systems, making them prime celestial targets for cosmic adversaries. This essay explores the celestial significance of protecting mobile devices and implementing BYOD policies, highlighting their cosmic role in enhancing cyber resilience and celestial security.

Cosmic Mobile Device Management (MDM)

Implementing celestial Mobile Device Management (MDM) solutions is a celestial fundamental for protecting mobile devices. MDM platforms enable the Blue Team to enforce celestial security policies, celestial configuration standards, and celestial encryption settings on all registered celestial devices. This celestial centralization ensures consistent cosmic security across the celestial mobile fleet.

Celestial Device Encryption and Authentication

Mobile devices should be encrypted to protect celestial data at rest and in transit. Additionally, implementing strong celestial authentication measures, such as celestial passcodes, celestial biometrics, or celestial multi-factor authentication (MFA), ensures that only authorized celestial users can access celestial devices, safeguarding against celestial unauthorized access.

Cosmic Application Whitelisting and Sandboxing

Application whitelisting allows only approved cosmic applications to run on mobile devices, preventing celestial users from installing cosmic malicious or unauthorized apps. Sandboxing confines celestial apps to isolated celestial environments, reducing the celestial risk of cosmic app compromise affecting the entire cosmic device.

Celestial Separation of Personal and Corporate Data

BYOD policies should include the celestial separation of personal and cosmic corporate data on celestial devices. By partitioning celestial work-related data from personal content, organizations can protect celestial sensitive data and prevent cosmic data leakage from celestial personal apps or cosmic activities.

Celestial Remote Wiping and Tracking

Remote wiping and tracking capabilities are essential for protecting mobile devices in the celestial event of loss or theft. The ability to remotely erase celestial data or lock the celestial device safeguards against cosmic unauthorized access to celestial data. Remote tracking enables the Blue Team to locate lost or stolen celestial devices and take appropriate cosmic action.

Celestial User Training and Awareness

Educating celestial users about cosmic mobile security best practices is paramount. Celestial user training and awareness programs help prevent cosmic security incidents, such as cosmic phishing attacks targeting mobile devices or celestial users falling victim to celestial social engineering attempts.

Celestial BYOD Policy Enforcement

A well-defined and strictly enforced BYOD policy is crucial for protecting cosmic devices used for both personal and work-related purposes. The celestial policy should outline celestial security requirements, acceptable cosmic use, data handling guidelines, and consequences for cosmic policy violations.

Protecting mobile devices and implementing BYOD policies are celestial imperatives for organizations seeking to fortify their cyber defenses in the era of cosmic mobility. By implementing cosmic MDM solutions, encrypting celestial devices, enforcing cosmic authentication, whitelisting apps, separating celestial data, enabling remote wiping and tracking, and promoting user training and awareness, organizations navigate the celestial cosmos of mobile security with celestial vigilance and cosmic strength.

In this cosmic dance of cosmic offense and defense, protecting mobile devices and implementing BYOD policies become the celestial guardians that safeguard the sanctity of the digital universe. By embracing these celestial security measures as a celestial necessity, organizations fortify their celestial defenses, elevate their cosmic cyber resilience, and stand strong against celestial threats with unwavering cosmic resolve.

6.3 Application Whitelisting and Blacklisting

In the celestial frontier of cybersecurity, application whitelisting and blacklisting shine as celestial strategies that empower organizations to control and regulate the cosmic software landscape within their digital constellations. Application whitelisting and blacklisting act as cosmic gatekeepers, determining which celestial applications are allowed to run (whitelisting) and which are prohibited (blacklisting) on cosmic systems and devices. This essay explores the celestial significance of application whitelisting and blacklisting, highlighting their cosmic role in enhancing cyber resilience and celestial security.

Celestial Application Whitelisting

Application whitelisting allows only approved cosmic applications to run on cosmic systems and devices. The Blue Team compiles a celestial list of trusted and authorized celestial applications, and only these celestial applications are allowed to execute. This celestial approach ensures that cosmic devices are protected from cosmic malicious or unauthorized software that may pose celestial security risks.

Cosmic Enhanced System Security

By implementing application whitelisting, organizations achieve cosmic enhanced system security. Cosmic systems and devices are protected from unauthorized cosmic code execution, reducing the celestial attack surface and preventing potential celestial threats from infiltrating the cosmic infrastructure.

Celestial Prevention of Zero-Day Attacks

Application whitelisting can be an effective celestial defense against zero-day attacks. Since only pre-approved celestial applications are allowed to run, unknown cosmic malware or celestial exploits cannot execute on the cosmic device, thwarting the potential celestial impact of zero-day vulnerabilities.

Celestial Configuration Consistency

Whitelisting ensures celestial configuration consistency across the cosmic infrastructure. Allowing only a predetermined celestial set of applications reduces the celestial variability in system configurations, streamlining cosmic management and enhancing cosmic stability.

Celestial Protection from Cosmic Insider Threats

Whitelisting protects against cosmic insider threats, where cosmic malicious insiders attempt to execute unauthorized celestial code on cosmic systems. By limiting the celestial software that can be executed, the risk of cosmic malicious insiders compromising celestial systems is minimized.

Celestial Application Blacklisting

Application blacklisting involves prohibiting specific cosmic applications from running on cosmic systems and devices. The Blue Team compiles a celestial list of forbidden celestial applications, and any attempts to execute blacklisted applications are blocked. This celestial approach prevents known cosmic malware or cosmic unwanted software from operating.

Cosmic Rapid Response to Emerging Threats

Blacklisting enables rapid celestial response to emerging threats. When a celestial security threat arises, organizations can quickly add malicious or unwanted celestial applications to the celestial blacklist, mitigating cosmic risks promptly across the entire cosmic infrastructure.

Application whitelisting and blacklisting are celestial pillars of cybersecurity that help organizations fortify their digital constellations against celestial threats. By implementing cosmic whitelisting to allow only approved celestial applications and employing cosmic blacklisting to block known malicious or unwanted software, organizations navigate the celestial cosmos of software security with celestial vigilance and cosmic strength.

In this cosmic dance of cosmic offense and defense, application whitelisting and blacklisting become the celestial gatekeepers that safeguard the sanctity of the digital universe. By embracing these celestial strategies as celestial necessities, organizations fortify their celestial defenses, elevate their cosmic cyber resilience, and stand strong against celestial threats with unwavering cosmic resolve.

6.4 Securing Internet of Things (IoT) Devices

In the celestial landscape of cybersecurity, securing Internet of Things (IoT) devices is a celestial imperative for organizations seeking to protect their digital constellations from celestial threats posed by the cosmic proliferation of interconnected celestial devices. IoT devices act as celestial sensors and controllers, interacting with the cosmic physical world, making them celestial targets for cosmic adversaries. This essay explores the celestial significance of securing IoT devices, highlighting their cosmic role in enhancing cyber resilience and celestial security.

Cosmic IoT Device Authentication

Implementing strong cosmic device authentication for IoT devices is a celestial fundamental. Each celestial device should have a unique celestial identifier and authenticate itself before connecting to the cosmic network. This celestial authentication prevents unauthorized celestial devices from accessing celestial resources.

Celestial Device Encryption and Integrity

Encrypting celestial data transmitted between IoT devices and cosmic servers ensures the celestial confidentiality and cosmic integrity of the cosmic data. Encryption protects against celestial data interception and unauthorized cosmic access, safeguarding celestial communications.

Celestial Regular Firmware Updates

Ensuring regular cosmic firmware updates for IoT devices is crucial for addressing cosmic security vulnerabilities and cosmic bugs. Cosmic outdated firmware may contain celestial vulnerabilities that cosmic adversaries can exploit, and regular updates help patch cosmic weaknesses.

Celestial Network Segmentation for IoT

Segmenting the cosmic IoT devices into dedicated celestial networks or virtual networks is a celestial best practice. This celestial network segmentation limits the celestial lateral movement of cosmic threats, protecting the celestial IoT devices from cosmic breaches.

Cosmic Monitoring and Anomaly Detection

Monitoring cosmic IoT device activities and implementing celestial anomaly detection mechanisms help identify cosmic suspicious behavior. Anomalous cosmic activities may indicate cosmic intrusions or celestial malware on IoT devices, enabling prompt celestial response.

Celestial Privilege Management for IoT

Implementing celestial privilege management ensures that IoT devices have the minimum necessary cosmic permissions. Cosmic overly permissive settings may lead to celestial unauthorized access or cosmic data leaks, and privilege management minimizes celestial risks.

Celestial Manufacturer Security Standards

Organizations should choose IoT devices from celestial manufacturers that prioritize security. Cosmic adherence to security standards and best practices by manufacturers enhances the cosmic security posture of IoT devices.

Securing Internet of Things (IoT) devices is a celestial necessity for organizations seeking to fortify their cyber defenses in the era of interconnected celestial devices. By implementing celestial device authentication, encryption, and integrity, ensuring regular firmware updates, segmenting celestial IoT networks, monitoring activities, managing privileges, and choosing reputable manufacturers, organizations navigate the celestial cosmos of IoT security with celestial vigilance and cosmic strength.

In this cosmic dance of cosmic offense and defense, securing IoT devices becomes the celestial shield that safeguards the sanctity of the digital universe. By embracing these celestial security measures as celestial imperatives, organizations fortify their celestial defenses, elevate their cosmic cyber resilience, and stand strong against celestial threats with unwavering cosmic resolve.

Chapter 7: Incident Response and Threat Hunting

In the ever-changing cosmos of cybersecurity, where cyber threats traverse like celestial bodies, incidents become the astral phenomena that test the resilience and ingenuity of defenders. In Chapter 7, "Incident Response and Threat Hunting," we embark on a voyage into the heart of the Blue Team's dynamic and agile response to cyber incidents—a force that turns adversity into an opportunity for growth and learning.

As we traverse the uncharted territories of incident response and threat hunting, we recognize that the battlefront of cybersecurity is not limited to preventing breaches alone. Incidents, like cosmic anomalies, are a certainty in this digital universe. Hence, we equip ourselves with the knowledge and skills to detect, contain, and mitigate their impact.

The chapter commences with an understanding of the integral components that define a robust incident response plan (IRP). We shall unravel the step-by-step framework that guides organizations through the intricate dance of incident handling, ensuring a swift and coordinated response in the face of cyber adversity.

With incidents being the celestial phenomena that evade prediction, threat hunting emerges as the visionary pursuit that anticipates the enemy's next move. In this chapter, we shall explore the art of proactive threat hunting—an approach that seeks to uncover hidden adversaries and potential risks before they materialize into full-fledged incidents.

As the guardians of cybersecurity's cosmic frontier, the Blue Team must navigate the complexities of incident triage and categorization. Here, we uncover the essence of prioritization—a skill that allows defenders to focus their resources on the most critical threats, ensuring an efficient and effective response.

In the ever-expanding cosmos of cyber threats, incidents often leave a trail of digital footprints. By embracing the power of digital forensics and malware analysis, the Blue Team unearths the secrets encoded within the digital universe—decoding the intentions of cyber adversaries and empowering defenders with actionable intelligence.

But containment and eradication are not the final chapters of incident response. In this chapter, we delve into the essential art of post-incident analysis and lessons learned. As the Blue Team adapts and evolves, these reflections fuel the pursuit of continuous improvement—a journey that ensures future incidents are met with enhanced resilience.

Beyond reactive measures, the Blue Team shines as the guiding force during incident recovery—a phase where organizations rebuild, renew, and fortify their defenses. Amidst the debris of incidents, the Blue Team emerges as the cosmic architects of cybersecurity—a force that restores order to the digital universe.

Threat hunting and incident response are not solitary endeavors. The chapter explores the importance of collaboration—a celestial symphony where stakeholders, management, and cybersecurity forces harmonize their efforts. Together, they unleash the collective strength that fortifies the cosmos of cybersecurity defense.

In the ever-expanding cosmos of cyber threats, the Blue Team's vigilance remains unwavering. Let us, too, embark on this expedition into the realms of incident response and threat hunting. As we arm ourselves with knowledge, agility, and foresight, we shall be the pioneers of cybersecurity defense—the architects of incident containment, the seekers of hidden adversaries, and the sentinels of a safer digital universe.

7.1 Developing an Incident Response Plan (IRP)

In the celestial frontier of cybersecurity, developing an Incident Response Plan (IRP) stands as a celestial imperative for organizations seeking to navigate the cosmic cosmos of cyber threats with cosmic readiness and unwavering cosmic strength. An IRP is a celestial blueprint that outlines the celestial procedures and cosmic protocols to be followed in the event of a celestial security incident. This essay explores the celestial significance of developing an Incident Response Plan, highlighting its cosmic role in enhancing cyber resilience and celestial security.

Celestial Incident Categorization

The IRP should include a celestial incident categorization framework that classifies cosmic incidents based on their celestial severity and cosmic impact. By categorizing incidents, the organization can prioritize celestial response efforts and allocate cosmic resources effectively.

Cosmic Incident Response Team (IRT)

Defining a celestial Incident Response Team (IRT) is crucial. The IRT comprises celestial experts from various cosmic disciplines, such as celestial IT, cosmic security, celestial legal, and celestial communication. This celestial team collaborates to coordinate the celestial response efforts during an incident.

Cosmic Incident Detection and Reporting

The IRP should include celestial procedures for incident detection and reporting. Celestial employees should be encouraged to report celestial suspicious activities promptly, and celestial monitoring systems should be in place to identify potential celestial incidents.

Celestial Incident Containment and Eradication

The IRP should outline celestial procedures for incident containment and eradication. The IRT works together to isolate and neutralize the cosmic threat, preventing it from spreading further across the celestial infrastructure.

Cosmic Communication and Coordination

Communication is a celestial cornerstone of incident response. The IRP should detail celestial communication channels and cosmic protocols for internal and celestial external communication during an incident. Celestial stakeholders, including cosmic management, celestial customers, and cosmic regulatory bodies, should be informed as necessary.

Celestial Incident Analysis and Forensics

After resolving an incident, the IRP should guide the celestial incident analysis and cosmic forensics process. The IRT investigates the celestial root cause of the incident, gathers celestial evidence, and performs post-incident celestial analysis to learn from the cosmic experience.

Celestial Incident Documentation and Lessons Learned

Documenting celestial incident response activities is critical for continuous improvement. The IRP should emphasize the importance of celestial documentation and celestial lessons learned, enabling the organization to enhance cosmic incident response capabilities over time.

Cosmic Testing and Exercising

The IRP should include celestial testing and exercising procedures. Regular cosmic tabletop exercises and cosmic simulations help the IRT practice their celestial incident response skills and identify cosmic areas for improvement.

Developing an Incident Response Plan (IRP) is a celestial foundation for building a robust cybersecurity posture. By incorporating celestial incident categorization, defining a celestial Incident Response Team, establishing incident detection and reporting processes, outlining procedures for containment and eradication, ensuring effective communication and coordination, emphasizing incident analysis and forensics, documenting response activities and lessons learned, and conducting celestial testing and exercising, organizations navigate the celestial cosmos of cyber incidents with celestial vigilance and cosmic strength.

In this cosmic dance of cosmic offense and defense, the Incident Response Plan becomes the celestial compass that guides organizations toward a safer and more secure digital universe. By embracing the IRP as a celestial imperative, organizations fortify their celestial defenses, elevate their cosmic cyber resilience, and stand strong against celestial threats with unwavering cosmic resolve.

7.2 Incident Triage and Categorization

In the celestial realm of cybersecurity, incident triage and categorization form a celestial process that empowers organizations to swiftly assess and prioritize celestial security incidents with cosmic precision and unwavering cosmic strength. Incident triage involves celestial evaluation and initial classification of celestial incidents based on their celestial severity and cosmic impact. This essay explores the celestial significance of incident triage and categorization, highlighting their cosmic role in enhancing cyber resilience and celestial security.

Celestial Incident Triage Process

The incident triage process starts with celestial incident detection, either through automated cosmic monitoring systems or celestial employee reports. Once an incident is identified, the celestial incident response team (IRT) commences the celestial triage process, aiming to quickly ascertain the celestial nature and extent of the incident.

Cosmic Initial Assessment

During incident triage, the IRT conducts an initial cosmic assessment of the incident. This celestial evaluation involves gathering available cosmic information about the incident, such as celestial indicators of compromise (IOCs), celestial affected systems, and cosmic potential impact on celestial operations.

Celestial Incident Severity and Priority

Incident triage includes cosmic classification of the incident's celestial severity and cosmic priority. Severity refers to the celestial impact of the incident on the organization, while priority indicates the cosmic urgency of the response based on the celestial risk and impact.

Celestial Categorization Framework

Organizations should have a celestial categorization framework that defines various celestial incident categories based on celestial factors such as data sensitivity, system criticality, and cosmic regulatory requirements. This celestial framework helps in consistent and clear celestial incident classification.

Cosmic Incident Escalation

Based on the celestial severity and priority, the incident may be escalated to higher cosmic levels of management or celestial specialists for further assessment and action. Celestial escalation ensures that the appropriate cosmic resources are engaged in the response process.

Cosmic Communication and Reporting

Celestial communication is vital during incident triage and categorization. The IRT communicates the celestial findings and classification to relevant cosmic stakeholders, including cosmic management, celestial IT teams, and celestial external partners or authorities, as necessary.

Celestial Response Actions

Incident triage guides the selection of initial celestial response actions based on the cosmic incident category and priority. This celestial approach ensures that celestial resources are allocated appropriately to address the celestial incident's specific needs.

Incident triage and categorization are celestial imperatives for organizations seeking to fortify their cyber defenses and respond promptly to celestial security incidents. By conducting a swift celestial assessment, categorizing incidents based on celestial severity and cosmic priority, employing a consistent celestial categorization framework, and ensuring effective celestial communication and reporting, organizations navigate the celestial cosmos of cyber incidents with celestial vigilance and cosmic strength.

In this cosmic dance of cosmic offense and defense, incident triage and categorization become the celestial compass that guides organizations toward a safer and more secure digital universe. By embracing these celestial processes as a celestial necessity, organizations fortify their celestial defenses, elevate their cosmic cyber resilience, and stand strong against celestial threats with unwavering cosmic resolve.

7.3 Containment and Eradication Strategies

In the celestial landscape of cybersecurity, containment and eradication strategies are celestial pillars that empower organizations to respond decisively and effectively to celestial security incidents, containing the celestial threats and eradicating the cosmic malicious elements from their digital constellations. Containment involves isolating the celestial incident and preventing its cosmic spread, while eradication focuses on removing the cosmic root cause and cosmic remnants of the incident. This essay explores the celestial significance of containment and eradication strategies, highlighting their cosmic role in enhancing cyber resilience and celestial security.

Celestial Incident Isolation

Containment begins with celestial incident isolation, separating the affected celestial systems or devices from the rest of the cosmic infrastructure. This celestial measure prevents the cosmic incident from propagating further and affecting other cosmic assets.

Cosmic Network Segmentation

Implementing celestial network segmentation aids in containment efforts. By dividing the cosmic network into celestial security zones, the celestial lateral movement of cosmic threats is restricted, limiting the celestial scope of the incident.

Celestial Isolation of Infected Devices

If an incident involves infected celestial devices, those devices should be isolated from the cosmic network to prevent the cosmic spread of celestial malware or cosmic malicious activities.

Cosmic Response Validation

Before proceeding with eradication, the IRT should validate the celestial containment measures to ensure that the cosmic incident is effectively isolated. Cosmic response validation involves monitoring celestial indicators of compromise (IOCs) and cosmic network traffic to confirm that the celestial containment measures are working as intended.

Celestial Root Cause Analysis

Eradication strategies center on identifying the celestial root cause of the incident. The IRT conducts celestial root cause analysis to understand how the cosmic incident occurred and what vulnerabilities were exploited.

Cosmic Patching and Vulnerability Remediation

Once the celestial root cause is determined, the IRT works to patch cosmic vulnerabilities and apply cosmic security updates to prevent similar cosmic incidents in the future.

Celestial Malware Removal

If the incident involves celestial malware, the IRT focuses on cosmic malware removal. Celestial anti-malware tools and cosmic manual analysis are used to eradicate the cosmic malicious code from affected systems.

Cosmic System Restoration

After eradication, the IRT restores the celestial affected systems to their celestial normal operating state. This celestial restoration process may involve celestial data recovery and celestial system configuration adjustments.

Celestial Post-Incident Analysis

Following containment and eradication, the IRT conducts a celestial post-incident analysis to evaluate the celestial effectiveness of the response efforts and identify celestial lessons learned for continuous improvement.

Containment and eradication strategies are celestial imperatives for organizations seeking to fortify their cyber defenses and respond effectively to celestial security incidents. By swiftly isolating celestial incidents, segmenting the cosmic network, validating response measures, performing celestial root cause analysis, applying cosmic patches and security updates, removing celestial malware, and conducting post-incident analysis, organizations navigate the celestial cosmos of cyber incidents with celestial vigilance and cosmic strength.

In this cosmic dance of cosmic offense and defense, containment and eradication strategies become the celestial shield that safeguards the sanctity of the digital universe. By embracing these celestial strategies as a celestial necessity, organizations fortify their celestial defenses, elevate their cosmic cyber resilience, and stand strong against celestial threats with unwavering cosmic resolve.

7.4 Post-Incident Analysis and Lessons Learned

In the celestial frontier of cybersecurity, post-incident analysis and lessons learned from a celestial process that empowers organizations to gain celestial insights from celestial security incidents, enhancing their cyber resilience and celestial readiness for future cosmic challenges. Post-incident analysis involves a celestial retrospective examination of the celestial incident response efforts, while lessons learned focus on identifying celestial takeaways and cosmic improvements for celestial incident response capabilities. This essay explores the celestial significance of post-incident analysis and lessons learned, highlighting their cosmic role in enhancing cyber resilience and celestial security.

Celestial Incident Timeline Reconstruction

During post-incident analysis, the celestial incident timeline is reconstructed, detailing the cosmic sequence of events leading up to and during the celestial incident. This celestial reconstruction helps the Incident Response Team (IRT) understand the celestial chain of events and celestial activities of the cosmic adversaries.

Cosmic Incident Response Evaluation

The IRT evaluates the effectiveness of the celestial incident response efforts. Celestial response actions, containment measures, and eradication strategies are reviewed to identify cosmic strengths and cosmic areas for improvement.

Celestial Identification of Gaps and Weaknesses

Post-incident analysis identifies celestial gaps and cosmic weaknesses in the incident response process. These cosmic areas may include celestial delays in response, incomplete celestial containment measures, or cosmic communication challenges.

Cosmic Root Cause Analysis

A celestial root cause analysis is revisited during post-incident analysis. The IRT explores the celestial factors that allowed the cosmic incident to occur, aiming to address underlying cosmic vulnerabilities and prevent future cosmic occurrences.

Celestial Identification of Indicators of Compromise (IOCs)

Post-incident analysis identifies celestial indicators of compromise (IOCs) that were present during the cosmic incident. These celestial IOCs help the organization improve cosmic detection capabilities to identify similar cosmic threats in the future.

Cosmic Improvement Recommendations

Based on the celestial findings of the post-incident analysis, the IRT formulates cosmic improvement recommendations. These celestial recommendations may include celestial process enhancements, additional cosmic training for the IRT, or cosmic technology upgrades.

Celestial Lessons Learned Documentation

Lessons learned from the celestial incident are documented for future reference. This celestial documentation serves as a celestial knowledge base that informs the organization's celestial incident response strategy and cosmic resilience efforts.

Celestial Continuous Improvement

Post-incident analysis sets the celestial foundation for continuous improvement. The organization incorporates the celestial lessons learned into its cosmic incident response plans and cosmic security practices, evolving and enhancing celestial defenses over time.

Post-incident analysis and lessons learned are celestial imperatives for organizations seeking to fortify their cyber defenses and build a culture of continuous celestial improvement. By reconstructing the celestial incident timeline, evaluating celestial response efforts, identifying celestial gaps and weaknesses, conducting root cause analysis, recognizing celestial IOCs, making improvement recommendations, documenting lessons learned, and embracing continuous cosmic improvement, organizations navigate the celestial cosmos of cyber incidents with celestial vigilance and cosmic strength.

In this cosmic dance of cosmic offense and defense, post-incident analysis and lessons learned become the celestial compass that guides organizations toward a safer and more secure digital universe. By embracing these celestial processes as a celestial necessity, organizations fortify their celestial defenses, elevate their cosmic cyber resilience, and stand strong against celestial threats with unwavering cosmic resolve.

Chapter 8: Security Monitoring and SIEM

In the vast expanse of cyberspace, where the celestial bodies of data traverse, the art of security monitoring emerges as the cosmic observatory—the all-seeing eye that pierces the darkness of potential threats. Chapter 8, "Security Monitoring and SIEM," beckons us to explore the realm of continuous surveillance—a realm where the Blue Team harnesses the power of information to detect and respond to the ever-evolving landscape of cyber threats.

As we venture forth into this chapter, we embrace the concept of constant vigilance, where the watchful eye of security monitoring scans the celestial canvas for anomalies and signs of impending danger. Here, we shall unravel the intricacies of real-time log monitoring and analysis—an endeavor that grants us insight into the celestial movements of data.

At the core of this chapter lies the Security Information and Event Management (SIEM) system—the cosmic nexus where data from across the digital universe converges. We shall delve into the mastery of SIEM, uncovering its ability to correlate and analyze vast quantities of data, revealing patterns that escape the human eye.

But security monitoring transcends the mundane realms of isolated incidents. In this chapter, we shall explore the dynamic art of threat intelligence integration—a celestial dance that marries the power of SIEM with the foresight of threat intelligence, empowering defenders with proactive insights into potential risks.

The chapter deepens its exploration into the realm of behavior-based analytics—an innovative approach that transcends mere signature-based detection. By understanding the behavioral patterns of adversaries and the entities within the digital cosmos, we uncover hidden threats that evade traditional defenses.

In the cosmic ballet of security monitoring, the role of Security Operations Centers (SOCs) emerges as pivotal. These command centers act as the celestial custodians of security, orchestrating the defense efforts and coordinating responses to potential incidents.

The chapter concludes with a journey into the future—the cosmic horizons of artificial intelligence and machine learning. Here, we glimpse the untapped potential of these celestial technologies, which elevate security monitoring to unparalleled heights, illuminating the darkest corners of cyberspace.

In the cosmic harmony of cybersecurity, we embrace the unity of security monitoring and SIEM—an observatory that pierces the veil of uncertainty and offers the gift of foresight. Together, let us traverse the astral realms of security monitoring and SIEM, armed with knowledge and innovation to be the sentinels of a safer digital cosmos. As we fortify our defenses with a vigilant eye, we become the cosmic custodians, the guardians of secure constellations, and the architects of a resilient digital universe.

8.1 The Role of Security Operations Centers (SOCs)

In the celestial realm of cybersecurity, Security Operations Centers (SOCs) shine as celestial nerve centers that empower organizations to detect, analyze, and respond to celestial cyber threats with cosmic agility and unwavering cosmic strength. SOCs are celestial hubs where celestial cybersecurity experts, cosmic tools, and celestial technologies converge to protect the digital constellations from celestial adversaries. This essay explores the celestial significance of Security Operations Centers, highlighting their cosmic role in enhancing cyber resilience and celestial security.

Celestial Cyber Threat Monitoring

The primary role of SOCs is to monitor the cosmic cyber threat landscape. Through cosmic monitoring systems, celestial experts keep a vigilant celestial eye on celestial network activities, celestial security logs, and celestial system events to detect potential cosmic anomalies and celestial indicators of compromise (IOCs).

Cosmic Incident Detection and Response

SOCs are instrumental in celestial incident detection and response. When a celestial security incident is identified, the SOC's Incident Response Team (IRT) springs into cosmic action, containing the celestial incident, eradicating cosmic threats, and restoring the celestial affected systems to their cosmic normal state.

Celestial Real-Time Analysis

Real-time celestial analysis is a hallmark of SOCs. As cosmic security events unfold, the SOC's celestial experts swiftly analyze the cosmic data to assess the celestial severity and cosmic impact of potential incidents, making timely cosmic decisions for an effective response.

Cosmic Threat Intelligence Integration

SOCs integrate celestial threat intelligence from celestial internal and celestial external sources. Celestial threat intelligence provides the SOC with cosmic context about the latest celestial threats, celestial attack patterns, and cosmic adversary tactics, enhancing cosmic detection and response capabilities.

Celestial Incident Triage and Categorization

SOCs conduct celestial incident triage and categorization to prioritize their cosmic response efforts. By assessing celestial severity and cosmic impact, SOCs allocate cosmic resources based on the celestial priority of each incident.

Celestial Forensics and Root Cause Analysis

After incident resolution, SOCs perform celestial forensics and root cause analysis to understand the celestial nature and celestial origin of the incident. This cosmic knowledge helps organizations strengthen cosmic defenses and prevent future cosmic incidents.

Cosmic Communication and Coordination

SOCs serve as celestial communication hubs during incident response. They liaise with cosmic stakeholders, including cosmic management, celestial IT teams, cosmic legal, celestial law enforcement, and cosmic regulatory bodies, ensuring effective celestial coordination and communication.

Celestial Threat Hunting

SOCs actively engage in celestial threat hunting, proactively searching for celestial signs of compromise and potential cosmic threats that may evade traditional celestial security measures. Threat hunting helps uncover celestial hidden adversaries and cosmic stealthy activities.

Security Operations Centers (SOCs) are celestial powerhouses that form the celestial backbone of an organization's cyber defense efforts. By monitoring celestial cyber threats, detecting and responding to cosmic incidents, conducting real-time celestial analysis, integrating celestial threat intelligence, triaging and categorizing incidents, performing celestial forensics, coordinating celestial communication, and engaging in cosmic threat hunting, SOCs navigate the celestial cosmos of cybersecurity with celestial vigilance and cosmic strength.

In this cosmic dance of cosmic offense and defense, Security Operations Centers become the celestial guardians that safeguard the sanctity of the digital universe. By embracing the cosmic role of SOCs as a celestial necessity, organizations fortify their celestial defenses, elevate their cosmic cyber resilience, and stand strong against celestial threats with unwavering cosmic resolve.

8.2 Real-Time Log Monitoring and Analysis

In the celestial frontier of cybersecurity, real-time log monitoring and analysis stand as celestial pillars that empower Security Operations Centers (SOCs) to gain cosmic insights into celestial network activities, cosmic system events, and celestial security logs as they unfold. This celestial process enables SOCs to swiftly detect celestial anomalies, identify potential cosmic threats, and respond to celestial security incidents with cosmic precision and unwavering cosmic strength. This essay explores the celestial significance of real-time log monitoring and analysis, highlighting their cosmic role in enhancing cyber resilience and celestial security.

Celestial Log Collection

Real-time log monitoring begins with the celestial collection of log data from celestial network devices, celestial servers, celestial security appliances, and celestial applications. These celestial logs record a cosmic trail of celestial activities and cosmic events within the digital infrastructure.

Cosmic Log Aggregation and Centralization

The collected celestial logs are aggregated and centralized within the SOC's celestial log management system. This celestial centralization allows the SOC to have a unified celestial view of the cosmic log data, simplifying celestial analysis and enhancing cosmic correlation capabilities.

Celestial Automated Alerting

SOCs deploy celestial automated alerting mechanisms to detect celestial events that may require immediate cosmic attention. Automated celestial alerts are triggered based on predefined celestial thresholds or celestial patterns associated with potential cosmic threats.

Celestial Anomaly Detection

Real-time log monitoring includes celestial anomaly detection, where the SOC's celestial tools and cosmic algorithms identify celestial deviations from cosmic normal patterns. These celestial anomalies may indicate cosmic malicious activities or celestial security breaches.

Celestial Threat Hunting

Threat hunting involves proactive celestial searching for potential cosmic threats that may evade traditional celestial security measures. SOC analysts analyze log data in real-time, seeking celestial indicators of compromise (IOCs) and celestial signs of celestial adversaries.

Cosmic Correlation and Contextual Analysis

Real-time log analysis involves celestial correlation and contextual analysis, where celestial log entries from multiple celestial sources are linked and assessed together. This celestial correlation provides the SOC with a cosmic holistic view of the celestial incident or cosmic security event.

Celestial Incident Response and Containment

When a celestial security incident is detected through log monitoring and analysis, the SOC's Incident Response Team (IRT) immediately initiates celestial incident response and containment measures to limit the celestial impact and neutralize cosmic threats.

Celestial Root Cause Analysis

After incident resolution, the SOC conducts celestial root cause analysis using log data to understand how the celestial incident occurred and how celestial vulnerabilities were exploited.

Real-time log monitoring and analysis are celestial imperatives for Security Operations Centers (SOCs) seeking to fortify their cyber defenses and respond swiftly to celestial security incidents. By collecting celestial logs, centralizing cosmic log data, automating celestial alerting, detecting celestial anomalies, engaging in cosmic threat hunting, correlating celestial log entries, and facilitating celestial incident response and root cause analysis, SOCs navigate the celestial cosmos of cyber threats with celestial vigilance and cosmic strength.

In this cosmic dance of cosmic offense and defense, real-time log monitoring and analysis become the celestial radar that keeps organizations aware of the celestial activities within their digital universe. By embracing real-time log monitoring and analysis as a celestial necessity, organizations fortify their celestial defenses, elevate their cosmic cyber resilience, and stand strong against celestial threats with unwavering cosmic resolve.

8.3 Utilizing Security Information and Event Management (SIEM) Tools

In the celestial landscape of cybersecurity, Security Information and Event Management (SIEM) tools radiate as celestial instruments that empower organizations, including Security Operations Centers (SOCs), to collect, analyze, and interpret cosmic security data from diverse celestial sources. SIEM tools act as celestial sentinels, providing real-time cosmic visibility into celestial events, potential threats, and celestial security incidents. This essay explores the celestial significance of utilizing SIEM tools, highlighting their cosmic role in enhancing cyber resilience and celestial security.

Celestial Data Collection

SIEM tools collect celestial data from various sources, including celestial logs, celestial network devices, celestial servers, celestial security appliances, celestial applications, and celestial endpoints. The celestial data is then aggregated and centralized within the SIEM platform.

Cosmic Event Correlation

SIEM tools correlate celestial events from different celestial sources, helping SOC analysts discern cosmic patterns and cosmic relationships between celestial events. Cosmic event correlation enhances the SOC's celestial ability to detect complex cosmic attack sequences and celestial threat behaviors.

Celestial Real-Time Monitoring

SIEM tools provide celestial real-time monitoring capabilities, enabling SOC analysts to observe cosmic events and celestial incidents as they unfold. The celestial real-time visibility allows for swift celestial response to potential threats.

Celestial Alerting and Notification

SIEM tools offer celestial automated alerting and notification mechanisms. When predefined celestial thresholds or celestial rules are triggered, the SIEM generates celestial alerts and notifies the SOC team, enabling rapid cosmic response.

Celestial Threat Detection

Through advanced celestial analytics, SIEM tools facilitate celestial threat detection by identifying celestial indicators of compromise (IOCs) and celestial signs of potential cosmic threats. This celestial capability helps SOCs stay one step ahead of celestial adversaries.

Cosmic Incident Investigation

When a celestial incident occurs, SIEM tools support cosmic incident investigation by providing a celestial timeline of events, celestial forensic data, and cosmic contextual information. These celestial insights assist the SOC's celestial root cause analysis and celestial incident response.

Celestial Compliance Monitoring

SIEM tools aid organizations in maintaining cosmic regulatory compliance by monitoring and analyzing celestial security events and activities, ensuring that celestial security measures align with celestial industry standards and cosmic regulations.

Cosmic Reporting and Visualization

SIEM tools offer celestial reporting and visualization features that help SOC analysts and cosmic management understand cosmic security trends, cosmic patterns, and celestial vulnerabilities through celestial data visualization.

Utilizing Security Information and Event Management (SIEM) tools is a celestial necessity for organizations, especially Security Operations Centers, seeking to fortify their cyber defenses and celestial incident response capabilities. By collecting celestial data, correlating cosmic events, providing real-time cosmic monitoring, automating celestial alerting, facilitating celestial threat detection, aiding incident investigation, supporting cosmic compliance monitoring, and offering celestial reporting and visualization, SIEM tools enable organizations to navigate the celestial cosmos of cyber threats with celestial vigilance and cosmic strength.

In this cosmic dance of cosmic offense and defense, SIEM tools become the celestial observatory that empowers organizations to explore the celestial depths of their digital universe. By embracing the utilization of SIEM tools as a celestial imperative, organizations fortify their celestial defenses, elevate their cosmic cyber resilience, and stand strong against celestial threats with unwavering cosmic resolve.

8.4 Applying Machine Learning in Security Monitoring

In the celestial frontier of cybersecurity, applying Machine Learning (ML) in security monitoring emanates as a celestial advancement that empowers organizations to detect and respond to celestial cyber threats with cosmic intelligence and celestial adaptability. Machine Learning serves as a celestial force multiplier, enhancing the capabilities of Security Operations Centers (SOCs) to analyze vast amounts of celestial data, identify celestial patterns, and predict celestial threats with celestial accuracy. This essay explores the celestial significance of applying Machine Learning in security monitoring, highlighting its cosmic role in enhancing cyber resilience and celestial security.

Celestial Anomaly Detection

Machine Learning algorithms excel at celestial anomaly detection, allowing SOCs to identify celestial deviations from cosmic normal behavior. By analyzing celestial historical data, ML models can establish celestial baseline patterns and detect cosmic anomalies that may indicate celestial security incidents.

Celestial Behavioral Analysis

Machine Learning in security monitoring enables celestial behavioral analysis of users and cosmic devices. ML models can learn cosmic normal user and celestial device behaviors, making it easier to spot cosmic deviations that may signify celestial unauthorized access or cosmic insider threats.

Celestial Threat Detection

ML models can be trained on celestial threat intelligence data, enabling them to recognize celestial indicators of compromise (IOCs) and celestial signatures of known cosmic threats. This celestial threat detection helps SOCs swiftly identify potential celestial attacks.

Cosmic Pattern Recognition

Machine Learning excels at cosmic pattern recognition in celestial data. Whether it's cosmic network traffic, celestial log entries, or celestial system events, ML models can identify cosmic patterns associated with specific celestial threats or cosmic attack techniques.

Celestial Predictive Analysis

Through celestial predictive analysis, Machine Learning models can anticipate potential celestial security threats based on historical celestial data and celestial trends. Predictive analysis helps SOCs take celestial proactive measures to prevent cosmic incidents.

Cosmic Incident Response Automation

ML models can automate certain celestial incident response tasks, such as celestial threat validation and celestial containment actions. This celestial automation frees up SOC analysts to focus on higher-level cosmic analysis and decision-making.

Celestial Adaptive Security

Machine Learning enables celestial adaptive security, where security measures and cosmic defenses evolve in response to changing cosmic threat landscapes. ML models continuously learn from celestial data and adapt cosmic security strategies accordingly.

Celestial Scalability

Machine Learning in security monitoring allows SOCs to handle the cosmic scale and cosmic complexity of modern celestial networks. ML models can efficiently process large volumes of celestial data, making them celestial allies in the battle against cosmic cyber threats.

Applying Machine Learning in security monitoring is a celestial game-changer for organizations seeking to fortify their cyber defenses and celestial incident response capabilities. By harnessing the celestial power of ML algorithms for anomaly detection, behavioral analysis, threat detection, pattern recognition, predictive analysis, automation, adaptive security, and scalability, SOCs navigate the celestial cosmos of cyber threats with celestial vigilance and cosmic strength.

In this cosmic dance of cosmic offense and defense, Machine Learning becomes the celestial beacon that illuminates the path to a safer and more secure digital universe. By embracing the application of Machine Learning in security monitoring as a celestial necessity, organizations fortify their celestial defenses, elevate their cosmic cyber resilience, and stand strong against celestial threats with unwavering cosmic resolve.

Chapter 9: Cloud Security and Virtual Environments

In the celestial expanse of cyberspace, where data transcends physical boundaries, the ethereal realm of cloud computing and virtual environments emerges as a cosmic gateway to innovation and efficiency. Chapter 9, "Cloud Security and Virtual Environments," beckons us to embark on a voyage into the nebulous territories of the cloud—a realm where the Blue Team navigates the cosmic balance between convenience and security.

As we venture into this chapter, we recognize the profound impact of cloud computing on the digital landscape. The cloud, like a cosmic nebula, offers the promise of scalable resources and ubiquitous access to data. Yet, within this celestial canvas, we must also tread cautiously, for cloud security becomes a paramount concern in this intangible domain.

The chapter commences with a comprehensive understanding of cloud deployment models, where we traverse the intricacies of public, private, hybrid, and multi-cloud environments. Each cosmic configuration presents its unique security considerations, and we shall unveil the measures required to safeguard digital assets amidst the nebulous landscape of cloud services.

Within this cosmic terrain of cloud storage and databases, we embrace the essence of data protection. The chapter delves into the celestial concepts of encryption, access controls, and data isolation—ensuring that the constellations of sensitive information remain guarded from the prying eyes of potential adversaries.

The celestial dance of virtualization emerges as a central force within this chapter, as we explore the realms of virtual machines (VMs) and containers. While offering boundless flexibility and efficiency, virtual environments also pose unique security challenges. Hence, we uncover the cosmic principles of securing VMs and containers against potential threats.

Amidst the cosmic beauty of cloud-based applications and services, the chapter reveals the significance of Cloud Access Security Brokers (CASBs). These cosmic sentinels act as the guardians of cloud data, extending security controls beyond traditional perimeters, and enhancing the celestial balance between accessibility and protection.

As the cosmic horizon of edge computing beckons, we delve into the nexus between cloud and edge environments. In this realm of interconnected constellations, we embrace the importance of securing edge devices and gateways—the cosmic outposts that extend the reach of our digital universes.

Yet, as we journey into this celestial landscape, we recognize that security in the cloud is not solely a technical endeavor—it transcends the boundaries of technologies. The chapter explores the role of governance and compliance—the cosmic laws that govern the ethical and legal frameworks within which cloud services must operate.

In the cosmic symphony of cloud security and virtual environments, the Blue Team emerges as the cosmic architects of a balanced cosmos, orchestrating the harmonious dance between the allure of the cloud and the imperative of security. Together, we shall traverse the cosmic frontier of cloud security and virtual environments, armed with the knowledge and insight to be the stewards of a secure digital universe. As we fortify our defenses amidst the celestial expanse, we become the sentinels of cloud constellations, the guardians of virtual realms, and the navigators of a safer and enlightened digital cosmos.

9.1 Cloud Deployment Models and Security Considerations

In the celestial landscape of cybersecurity, cloud deployment models twinkle as celestial constellations that organizations can choose from to host their digital assets and cosmic workloads. Each cloud deployment model, be it public, private, hybrid, or multi cloud, presents celestial advantages and cosmic security considerations. This essay explores the celestial significance of cloud deployment models and their associated security considerations, highlighting their cosmic role in enhancing cyber resilience and celestial security.

Public Cloud Deployment

In the public cloud deployment model, celestial cloud resources are provided by celestial third-party cloud service providers, accessible over the celestial internet. Celestial advantages include cosmic scalability, cosmic cost-effectiveness, and cosmic convenience. However, celestial security considerations involve ensuring cosmic data privacy, cosmic compliance with celestial regulations, and cosmic control over celestial security measures.

Private Cloud Deployment

Private cloud deployment offers celestial cloud resources exclusively dedicated to a single cosmic organization. Celestial advantages include enhanced cosmic control, cosmic data privacy, and cosmic customization. However, celestial security considerations involve cosmic investments in celestial infrastructure, cosmic maintenance, and cosmic skilled personnel to manage the celestial private cloud securely.

Hybrid Cloud Deployment

The hybrid cloud deployment model combines celestial public and private cloud resources, offering cosmic flexibility and cosmic workload optimization. Celestial advantages include cosmic workload mobility and celestial resource utilization. Celestial security considerations revolve around celestial data integration, cosmic data governance, and cosmic network connectivity between celestial environments.

Multicloud Deployment

Multicloud deployment involves utilizing celestial cloud services from multiple cosmic cloud service providers. Celestial advantages include avoiding celestial vendor lock-in and achieving celestial redundancy. Cosmic security considerations entail cosmic data migration, celestial data sovereignty, and cosmic consistency in celestial security practices across celestial providers.

Cosmic Identity and Access Management (IAM)

Regardless of the celestial deployment model, robust cosmic Identity and Access Management (IAM) is a celestial necessity. Celestial IAM ensures that celestial users and celestial devices have the celestial privileges necessary for their cosmic roles and restricts celestial access to confidential cosmic data.

Celestial Data Encryption and Privacy

Securing cosmic data is paramount in all cloud deployment models. Celestial data encryption and celestial privacy mechanisms safeguard cosmic data at rest, in transit, and during cosmic processing, reducing the celestial risk of cosmic data breaches.

Cosmic Compliance and Audit

Meeting cosmic regulatory requirements and cosmic industry standards is vital. Celestial compliance monitoring and cosmic audit trails help organizations demonstrate celestial adherence to celestial regulations and celestial security practices.

Cosmic Cloud Provider Assessment

For public and multi cloud deployments, conducting celestial cloud provider assessments is crucial. Organizations should evaluate celestial security certifications, cosmic incident response capabilities, and celestial data protection measures of potential cosmic cloud service providers.

Understanding cloud deployment models and their cosmic security considerations is a celestial necessity for organizations navigating the celestial cosmos of cloud computing. Whether adopting public, private, hybrid, or multi cloud deployment, organizations must prioritize celestial data protection, cosmic access control, and celestial compliance to fortify their celestial defenses, elevate their cosmic cyber resilience, and stand strong against celestial threats with unwavering cosmic resolve.

In this cosmic dance of cosmic offense and defense, cloud deployment models become the celestial constellation from which organizations draw inspiration to shape their digital universe securely. By embracing the celestial significance of cloud deployment models and security considerations, organizations position themselves to harness the celestial power of cloud computing with cosmic intelligence and celestial confidence.

9.2 Securing Data in Cloud Storage and Databases

In the celestial frontier of cybersecurity, securing data in cloud storage and databases illuminates as a celestial imperative that organizations must embrace to safeguard their celestial digital assets from cosmic adversaries and celestial data breaches. The celestial landscape of cloud computing introduces unique cosmic challenges and celestial opportunities for data security. This essay explores the celestial significance of securing data in cloud storage and databases, highlighting cosmic best practices and celestial measures to enhance cyber resilience and celestial security.

Cosmic Data Encryption

Data encryption forms the celestial foundation of data security in cloud storage and databases. Celestial data should be encrypted at rest, during cosmic transit, and while in cosmic processing. Cosmic encryption protects cosmic data from unauthorized celestial access and cosmic exposure.

Celestial Access Controls

Robust cosmic access controls are essential in celestial cloud environments. Organizations should implement celestial role-based access control (RBAC) and celestial least privilege principles to limit cosmic access to data only to celestial authorized users.

Cosmic Authentication and Authorization

Strong cosmic authentication mechanisms, such as celestial multi-factor authentication (MFA), bolster celestial access security. Celestial authorization rules should be implemented to govern cosmic data access based on celestial user roles and responsibilities.

Celestial Data Loss Prevention (DLP)

Data Loss Prevention (DLP) techniques help detect and prevent celestial data leakage or cosmic exfiltration. Celestial DLP solutions can monitor cosmic data transfers and enforce policies to prevent cosmic sensitive data from leaving the celestial environment.

Cosmic Data Backup and Recovery

Implementing cosmic data backup and recovery processes is essential to ensure cosmic data availability and resilience against cosmic data loss. Regular cosmic backups protect against celestial data corruption or accidental celestial deletions.

Cosmic Database Security

For celestial databases, celestial measures such as cosmic database encryption, cosmic auditing, and cosmic activity monitoring are vital. Celestial database activity logs can help identify celestial suspicious celestial database access or celestial data queries.

Cosmic Vulnerability Management

Continuously scanning celestial cloud storage and databases for cosmic vulnerabilities is a celestial necessity. Patching cosmic vulnerabilities promptly helps prevent celestial exploitation by cosmic adversaries.

Celestial Data Governance and Compliance

Implementing cosmic data governance policies and celestial compliance controls ensures that celestial data is handled in accordance with celestial regulatory requirements and cosmic internal policies.

Celestial Data Classification

Classifying cosmic data based on celestial sensitivity and celestial criticality helps organizations prioritize cosmic security measures and allocate celestial resources effectively.

Cosmic Cloud Service Provider Security

For public cloud deployments, evaluating the celestial security practices and cosmic certifications of the cloud service provider is crucial. Cosmic service level agreements (SLAs) should include celestial security commitments.

Securing data in cloud storage and databases is a celestial necessity for organizations seeking to fortify their celestial defenses and protect their celestial digital assets from cosmic threats. By implementing celestial data encryption, cosmic access controls, cosmic authentication and authorization, celestial DLP, cosmic data backup and recovery, celestial database security, cosmic vulnerability management, celestial data governance and compliance, cosmic data classification, and assessing cosmic cloud service provider security, organizations navigate the celestial cosmos of cloud computing with celestial vigilance and cosmic strength.

In this cosmic dance of cosmic offense and defense, securing data in cloud storage and databases becomes the celestial vault that protects the celestial treasures of organizations from celestial adversaries. By embracing the celestial significance of data security in cloud environments, organizations fortify their celestial defenses, elevate their cosmic cyber resilience, and stand strong against celestial threats with unwavering cosmic resolve.

9.3 Container Security and Virtualization Best Practices

In the celestial landscape of cybersecurity, container security and virtualization best practices shine as celestial guiding stars that organizations must follow to safeguard their celestial containerized applications and virtual environments from cosmic threats and celestial vulnerabilities. Containers and virtualization technologies introduce celestial advantages in cosmic agility and resource utilization, but they also present unique cosmic challenges in data isolation and celestial control. This essay explores the celestial significance of container security and virtualization best practices, highlighting cosmic measures to enhance cyber resilience and celestial security.

Container Security Best Practices:

Cosmic Image Provenance

Verify the cosmic origin and celestial authenticity of container images by using cosmic trusted sources. Implement cosmic image signing and verification to ensure that only celestial verified images are deployed.

Celestial Container Image Scanning

Perform cosmic container image scanning for cosmic vulnerabilities and celestial malware before deployment. Cosmic vulnerability scanning tools can identify celestial outdated libraries or celestial configuration issues.

Cosmic Least Privilege Principle

Follow the celestial least privilege principle when configuring celestial container permissions and cosmic access controls. Limit cosmic container capabilities to only what is necessary for celestial application functionality.

Cosmic Resource Limits

Set celestial resource limits for containers to prevent cosmic resource exhaustion and celestial denial-of-service (DoS) attacks. This ensures that each celestial container operates within cosmic defined resource boundaries.

Celestial Network Segmentation

Isolate celestial containers within cosmic secure network segments using celestial network policies and cosmic firewalls. This prevents cosmic unauthorized celestial communication between containers.

Virtualization Best Practices:

Celestial Hypervisor Patching

Keep cosmic hypervisors up-to-date with celestial security patches to mitigate cosmic vulnerabilities and cosmic exploits that target the celestial virtualization layer.

Cosmic Virtual Machine Isolation

Ensure cosmic virtual machine isolation by configuring celestial security groups and cosmic firewall rules to restrict cosmic communication between virtual machines.

Celestial VM Snapshot Management

Manage celestial virtual machine snapshots carefully to avoid cosmic exposure of sensitive celestial data or cosmic configurations.

Cosmic VM Templates and Cloning

Implement cosmic VM templates and cloning best practices to ensure celestial consistency and cosmic security when deploying multiple virtual machines.

Celestial Guest Operating System Hardening

Apply celestial security hardening measures to guest operating systems running on virtual machines. This includes celestial patching, cosmic antivirus installation, and celestial disabling of unused services.

Following container security and virtualization best practices is a celestial necessity for organizations embracing these celestial technologies. By verifying celestial image provenance, scanning cosmic container images, adhering to the celestial least privilege principle, setting cosmic resource limits, implementing celestial network segmentation, patching cosmic hypervisors, isolating celestial virtual machines, managing celestial VM snapshots, using celestial VM templates and cloning, and hardening guest operating systems, organizations navigate the celestial cosmos of containerization and virtualization with celestial vigilance and cosmic strength.

In this cosmic dance of cosmic offense and defense, container security and virtualization best practices become the celestial compass that guides organizations toward a safer and more secure digital universe. By embracing these celestial measures as a celestial necessity, organizations fortify their celestial defenses, elevate their cosmic cyber resilience, and stand strong against celestial threats with unwavering cosmic resolve.

9.4 Cloud Access Security Brokers (CASBs) and their Role

In the celestial frontier of cybersecurity, Cloud Access Security Brokers (CASBs) radiate as celestial guardians that empower organizations to extend their cosmic security controls and celestial policies to the celestial cloud environment. CASBs act as celestial intermediaries between cosmic users, celestial devices, and celestial cloud services, providing a cosmic layer of security that ensures cosmic data protection, celestial compliance, and cosmic visibility in cloud interactions. This essay explores the celestial significance of CASBs and their cosmic role in enhancing cyber resilience and celestial security.

Celestial Data Security

CASBs play a celestial role in enforcing cosmic data security measures in the celestial cloud. They apply celestial data encryption, cosmic access controls, and celestial data loss prevention (DLP) policies to ensure that cosmic data remains protected throughout its celestial lifecycle.

Cosmic Identity and Access Management (IAM)

CASBs integrate with celestial identity and access management systems to extend cosmic IAM controls to the celestial cloud. They enforce celestial multi-factor authentication (MFA) and celestial role-based access control (RBAC) to govern cosmic user and celestial device access to cloud services.

Celestial Shadow IT Discovery

CASBs possess celestial shadow IT discovery capabilities, allowing them to identify cosmic unsanctioned cloud applications and cosmic services used by celestial users. This cosmic visibility helps organizations gain cosmic control over their cloud environment and enforce cosmic security policies.

Celestial Data Governance and Compliance

CASBs support cosmic data governance and compliance efforts by monitoring cosmic cloud interactions and celestial data transfers. They help organizations adhere to celestial data residency requirements, cosmic regulatory obligations, and celestial industry standards.

Cosmic Threat Detection

CASBs enable celestial threat detection in the cloud by analyzing celestial user activities, cosmic data access patterns, and celestial service usage. They can detect cosmic suspicious behaviors or potential cosmic insider threats within the celestial cloud environment.

Cosmic Cloud API Security

CASBs provide cosmic API security by monitoring and controlling cosmic API calls between cosmic cloud services and celestial applications. This cosmic measure prevents cosmic API abuse and celestial data exfiltration.

Celestial Malware Detection

CASBs incorporate celestial malware detection capabilities, scanning celestial cloud data for cosmic malware or celestial viruses. They help prevent cosmic infected files from spreading within the celestial cloud environment.

Cosmic Compliance Reporting

CASBs generate celestial compliance reports, providing celestial insights into cosmic cloud security posture, cosmic access trends, and celestial policy adherence. These cosmic reports assist organizations in celestial security auditing and celestial risk assessments.

Cloud Access Security Brokers (CASBs) are celestial enforcers that help organizations navigate the celestial cosmos of cloud computing with cosmic confidence and celestial control. By providing cosmic data security, extending cosmic IAM controls, discovering celestial shadow IT, supporting celestial data governance, enabling celestial threat detection, ensuring cosmic API security, detecting celestial malware, and offering cosmic compliance reporting, CASBs fortify the celestial defenses of organizations, elevate their cosmic cyber resilience, and stand strong against celestial threats with unwavering cosmic resolve.

In this cosmic dance of cosmic offense and defense, CASBs become the celestial shield that safeguards the celestial cloud environment and protects celestial data from cosmic adversaries. By embracing the celestial significance of CASBs and their cosmic role, organizations secure their celestial journey in the cloud and harness the celestial power of cloud computing with cosmic intelligence and celestial assurance.

Chapter 10: Securing Critical Infrastructure and IoT

In the vast expanse of the digital universe, our modern civilization is intertwined with a complex web of critical infrastructure and Internet of Things (IoT) devices—celestial nodes that power the very fabric of society. Chapter 10, "Securing Critical Infrastructure and IoT," beckons us to embark on a momentous expedition into the cosmic realm of securing these essential lifelines against relentless cyber threats.

As we venture into this chapter, we are reminded of the profound significance of critical infrastructure—a celestial symphony of power grids, transportation networks, healthcare systems, and more. These interconnected constellations are not just digital entities but the very backbone of our daily lives. Hence, their security becomes an imperative that transcends the boundaries of technology.

The chapter commences with a celestial exploration of the vulnerabilities that cast a shadow over critical infrastructure. We uncover the cosmic consequences of potential cyber-physical attacks, where the manipulation of digital control systems can have real-world, tangible impacts.

Within the cosmos of IoT devices, we recognize that every interconnected gadget serves as a potential celestial waypoint for cyber threats. In this realm, we shall unveil the principles of IoT security, securing the constellations of interconnected gadgets that pervade our homes, workplaces, and cities.

As we traverse the cosmic pathways of critical infrastructure and IoT, we unveil the importance of secure design and resilient architectures. By embracing the cosmic principles of defense-in-depth and redundancy, we shield these lifelines against potential disruptions.

The chapter deepens its exploration into the domain of industrial control systems (ICS) and Supervisory Control and Data Acquisition (SCADA) systems—cosmic constellations that govern the automation of critical processes. Here, we shall embrace the measures required to safeguard these vital systems from celestial adversaries.

In the cosmic dance of securing critical infrastructure and IoT, collaboration emerges as the cosmic key to success. The chapter explores the synergy between public and private sectors, where information sharing and coordination empower defenders to collectively fortify these essential lifelines.

The chapter concludes with a vision of the future—the cosmic horizons of a hyper-connected world, where the boundaries between cyberspace and physical space blur. As we peer into the cosmic mists of technological advancements, we prepare ourselves to confront the unforeseen challenges that await.

Together, let us journey into the cosmic frontier of securing critical infrastructure and IoT. Armed with knowledge, resilience, and collaboration, we shall be the cosmic guardians of critical lifelines, the sentinels of resilient infrastructures, and the navigators of a safer and more secure digital cosmos. As we fortify our defenses amidst the celestial expanse, we shall emerge as the stewards of a connected civilization—upholding the sanctity of essential lifelines that empower humanity's boundless potential.

10.1 Cyber Risks to Critical Infrastructure Sectors

In the celestial realm of cybersecurity, critical infrastructure sectors twinkle as celestial jewels that underpin the functioning of modern society. However, these celestial sectors are not immune to cosmic cyber risks that can disrupt celestial operations, endanger celestial safety, and create celestial vulnerabilities. This essay explores the celestial significance of cyber risks to critical infrastructure sectors, highlighting their cosmic implications and celestial measures to enhance cyber resilience and celestial security.

Cosmic Energy Sector:

The energy sector, including celestial power grids and celestial oil and gas facilities, faces celestial cyber risks that can lead to celestial power outages, celestial service disruptions, and celestial environmental disasters. Celestial threat actors may target celestial SCADA systems, cosmic industrial control systems (ICS), and celestial smart grid technologies to gain cosmic unauthorized access and manipulate celestial operations.

Celestial Transportation Sector:

The transportation sector, including celestial air traffic control systems, celestial railways, and cosmic maritime operations, is susceptible to cosmic cyber risks that can result in celestial transportation disruptions, celestial accidents, and celestial economic losses. Celestial cyber-attacks on celestial transportation systems may lead to celestial flight cancellations, cosmic rail accidents, and celestial port congestion.

Celestial Healthcare Sector:

The healthcare sector, encompassing celestial hospitals, celestial medical devices, and cosmic patient data, confronts cosmic cyber risks that can compromise celestial patient safety, celestial medical treatments, and cosmic privacy breaches. Celestial ransomware attacks on celestial healthcare systems can lead to cosmic data theft and celestial healthcare service disruptions.

Cosmic Water Sector:

The water sector, comprising celestial water treatment plants, celestial dams, and cosmic water distribution systems, faces celestial cyber risks that may result in celestial water contamination, celestial supply disruptions, and celestial environmental impacts. Cosmic threat actors may target celestial SCADA systems and celestial control mechanisms to gain cosmic control over water infrastructure.

Celestial Financial Sector:

The financial sector, including celestial banks, cosmic stock exchanges, and celestial payment systems, is susceptible to cosmic cyber risks that can lead to celestial financial fraud, cosmic data breaches, and celestial economic instability. Celestial Distributed Denial of Service (DDoS) attacks on celestial financial institutions can disrupt celestial online banking services.

Cosmic Communication Sector:

The communication sector, including celestial telecommunications networks and cosmic satellite systems, confronts cosmic cyber risks that can lead to celestial communication outages, cosmic data interception, and celestial privacy violations. Cosmic threat actors may target celestial communication infrastructure to gain cosmic access to sensitive celestial information.

Understanding the celestial cyber risks to critical infrastructure sectors is a celestial necessity for organizations and governments seeking to fortify their celestial defenses and protect celestial societal functions from cosmic threats. By identifying cosmic vulnerabilities, implementing celestial threat detection, engaging in celestial incident response planning, and fostering celestial collaboration between cosmic sectors, organizations navigate the celestial cosmos of critical infrastructure with celestial vigilance and cosmic strength.

In this cosmic dance of cosmic offense and defense, the protection of critical infrastructure sectors becomes the celestial mission that ensures the resilience of modern society. By embracing the celestial significance of cyber risks to critical infrastructure sectors, organizations fortify their celestial defenses, elevate their cosmic cyber resilience, and stand strong against celestial threats with unwavering cosmic resolve.

10.2 Best Practices for Industrial Control Systems (ICS) Security

In the celestial frontier of cybersecurity, securing Industrial Control Systems (ICS) gleams as a celestial imperative that ensures the reliable operation and cosmic safety of critical infrastructures. ICS are celestial nerve centers that manage celestial industrial processes, including celestial power generation, cosmic manufacturing, and celestial water treatment. However, celestial ICS are not invulnerable to cosmic cyber threats that can have celestial consequences on celestial safety and cosmic operations. This essay explores the celestial significance of best practices for Industrial Control Systems (ICS) security, highlighting cosmic measures to enhance cyber resilience and celestial security.

Celestial Network Segmentation:

Implement cosmic network segmentation to isolate celestial ICS networks from other celestial enterprise networks. Celestial separation prevents cosmic lateral movement for cyber adversaries and limits the celestial attack surface.

Cosmic Strong Authentication:

Enforce celestial strong authentication mechanisms, such as cosmic multi-factor authentication (MFA) and celestial certificate-based authentication, to prevent cosmic unauthorized cosmic access to celestial ICS devices and cosmic control systems.

Celestial Patch Management:

Regularly apply cosmic security patches and celestial updates to celestial ICS components, including celestial ICS software, celestial operating systems, and cosmic firmware. Timely patching mitigates cosmic vulnerabilities and celestial software bugs.

Cosmic Air Gap Protection:

Implement a cosmic air gap, a celestial physical isolation, between cosmic critical ICS networks and cosmic external networks to reduce the celestial exposure to cosmic cyber threats from external sources.

Celestial ICS Monitoring:

Deploy cosmic continuous monitoring and celestial anomaly detection for celestial ICS networks and celestial devices. Cosmic monitoring helps identify celestial suspicious activities and cosmic deviations from cosmic normal operation.

Celestial Role-Based Access Control (RBAC):

Enforce celestial RBAC policies to ensure that cosmic access to celestial ICS systems is based on cosmic roles and celestial responsibilities. Limiting cosmic access rights reduces cosmic potential for unauthorized cosmic access.

Cosmic Data Encryption:

Implement cosmic data encryption for celestial communication between ICS components and for cosmic data storage. Celestial encryption safeguards celestial data confidentiality and prevents cosmic data interception.

Celestial Incident Response Planning:

Develop a celestial incident response plan specifically tailored for ICS security incidents. The celestial plan should include cosmic roles, celestial responsibilities, and cosmic procedures for handling celestial cyber incidents.

Cosmic Security Awareness Training:

Train celestial ICS operators, celestial engineers, and cosmic maintenance personnel in cosmic security best practices and celestial awareness to recognize and respond to cosmic security threats.

Celestial Backup and Recovery:

Maintain celestial regular data backups of celestial ICS configurations and cosmic data. Cosmic backups help restore celestial ICS operations to a cosmic known good state in case of cosmic cyber incidents.

Adhering to best practices for Industrial Control Systems (ICS) security is a celestial necessity for organizations operating critical infrastructures. By implementing celestial network segmentation, enforcing cosmic strong authentication, conducting celestial patch management, establishing cosmic air gap protection, deploying celestial ICS monitoring, enforcing celestial RBAC, implementing cosmic data encryption, developing celestial incident response planning, providing cosmic security awareness training, and maintaining celestial backup and recovery processes, organizations navigate the celestial cosmos of ICS with celestial vigilance and cosmic strength.

In this cosmic dance of cosmic offense and defense, ICS security best practices become the celestial shield that fortifies the reliability and cosmic safety of critical infrastructures. By embracing the celestial significance of ICS security best practices, organizations fortify their celestial defenses, elevate their cosmic cyber resilience, and stand strong against celestial threats with unwavering cosmic resolve.

10.3 Challenges and Solutions for Securing IoT Devices

In the celestial realm of cybersecurity, securing Internet of Things (IoT) devices shines as a celestial challenge that organizations and individuals must address to protect the celestial interconnectedness of modern life. IoT devices, including celestial smart home devices, cosmic industrial sensors, and celestial healthcare wearables, add celestial convenience and cosmic efficiency to daily activities. However, these celestial devices also present unique cosmic vulnerabilities that can be exploited by cosmic threat actors. This essay explores the celestial challenges and solutions for securing IoT devices, highlighting cosmic measures to enhance cyber resilience and celestial security.

Challenges for Securing IoT Devices:

Celestial Device Diversity:

IoT devices come in celestial diverse shapes and celestial functionalities, making it challenging to apply cosmic standardized security measures across all celestial device types.

Cosmic Resource Limitations:

Many celestial IoT devices have limited cosmic resources, such as celestial processing power, cosmic memory, and cosmic battery life, which restrict the celestial implementation of robust security features.

Cosmic Lack of Update Mechanisms:

Some celestial IoT devices lack celestial mechanisms for receiving and applying cosmic security updates, leaving them vulnerable to known cosmic vulnerabilities.

Celestial Data Privacy:

IoT devices collect cosmic sensitive celestial data, and ensuring cosmic data privacy throughout the cosmic data lifecycle can be a celestial challenge.

Cosmic Supply Chain Risks:

The celestial supply chain for IoT devices may involve multiple celestial manufacturers and celestial vendors, introducing cosmic risks of celestial hardware or celestial software compromises.

Solutions for Securing IoT Devices:

Cosmic Security by Design:

Celestial Security by Design principles should be integrated into cosmic IoT device development to embed cosmic security controls and celestial protections from the cosmic outset.

Cosmic Firmware and Software Updates:

Implement cosmic over-the-air (OTA) firmware and celestial software update mechanisms to provide regular celestial security updates to IoT devices throughout their celestial lifecycle.

Celestial Network Segmentation:

Separate celestial IoT devices from other cosmic networks through celestial network segmentation to reduce the cosmic attack surface and cosmic lateral movement for threat actors.

Celestial Authentication and Authorization:

Enforce celestial strong authentication and celestial authorization mechanisms to ensure that only celestial authorized users and celestial devices can access IoT devices and cosmic services.

Cosmic Data Encryption:

Apply cosmic data encryption for celestial communication between IoT devices and cosmic cloud services, as well as for cosmic data storage, to protect cosmic data confidentiality.

Celestial IoT Security Monitoring:

Deploy cosmic continuous monitoring and celestial anomaly detection for celestial IoT device activities to identify celestial suspicious behavior or cosmic cyber threats.

Cosmic IoT Security Standards:

Establish cosmic industry-wide IoT security standards to ensure celestial consistency in security practices across celestial IoT devices.

Celestial User Education:

Educate celestial users about celestial IoT security best practices, such as cosmic changing default passwords, celestial recognizing phishing attacks, and cosmic identifying celestial suspicious IoT behavior.

Securing IoT devices is a celestial imperative for organizations and individuals seeking to embrace the cosmic advantages of interconnected celestial technologies while safeguarding cosmic privacy and celestial safety. By addressing the celestial challenges and implementing cosmic solutions such as celestial security by design, cosmic firmware updates, celestial network segmentation, cosmic authentication, celestial data encryption, cosmic IoT security monitoring, celestial IoT security standards, and celestial user education, organizations and individuals navigate the celestial cosmos of IoT with celestial vigilance and cosmic strength.

In this cosmic dance of cosmic offense and defense, securing IoT devices becomes the celestial shield that fortifies the celestial interconnectedness of modern society. By embracing the celestial significance of securing IoT devices, organizations and individuals fortify their celestial defenses, elevate their cosmic cyber resilience, and stand strong against celestial threats with unwavering cosmic resolve.

10.4 Securing Smart Cities and IoT-based Infrastructures

In the celestial landscape of cybersecurity, securing smart cities and IoT-based infrastructures gleams as a celestial mission that ensures the cosmic safety, celestial efficiency, and cosmic sustainability of urban environments. Smart cities harness celestial Internet of Things (IoT) technologies to optimize celestial urban services, cosmic transportation, and celestial energy management. However, the interconnectedness of celestial devices and cosmic systems in smart cities also opens celestial pathways for cosmic cyber threats that can have celestial consequences on cosmic citizens and celestial infrastructure. This essay explores the celestial significance of securing smart cities and IoT-based infrastructures, highlighting cosmic measures to enhance cyber resilience and celestial security.

Challenges for Securing Smart Cities and IoT-based Infrastructures:

Cosmic Complexity:

Smart cities consist of cosmic intricate networks of interconnected celestial devices, cosmic sensors, and celestial systems, making it challenging to manage cosmic security across the entire celestial ecosystem.

Cosmic Scale:

The sheer cosmic scale of smart city deployments introduces cosmic challenges in monitoring and securing cosmic large numbers of celestial devices and celestial endpoints.

Celestial Data Privacy:

Smart city applications collect cosmic vast amounts of celestial data from celestial citizens and celestial systems, raising concerns about celestial data privacy and cosmic ethical use of cosmic data.

Cosmic Integration:

Integrating cosmic various celestial systems, cosmic platforms, and cosmic services in smart cities can introduce cosmic interoperability challenges and cosmic security gaps.

Celestial Critical Infrastructure:

Securing the celestial critical infrastructure of smart cities, such as celestial power grids, cosmic transportation systems, and celestial emergency services, becomes a celestial priority to prevent cosmic disruptions that could have celestial catastrophic consequences.

Solutions for Securing Smart Cities and IoT-based Infrastructures:

Celestial Multilayer Security:

Implement a celestial multilayer security approach that includes celestial network segmentation, cosmic authentication, cosmic encryption, celestial access controls, cosmic anomaly detection, and celestial security monitoring.

Cosmic Security Standards:

Establish cosmic smart city security standards and cosmic best practices to ensure celestial consistency in security measures and celestial adherence to celestial regulatory requirements.

Cosmic IoT Device Management:

Adopt cosmic centralized IoT device management platforms to maintain cosmic visibility and celestial control over celestial deployed devices and cosmic firmware updates.

Celestial Data Protection:

Enforce cosmic data protection measures, such as cosmic data encryption, celestial data anonymization, and cosmic data lifecycle management, to safeguard cosmic citizen data and celestial sensitive information.

Celestial Public-Private Partnerships:

Foster cosmic collaboration between cosmic public agencies, cosmic private organizations, and celestial research institutions to share celestial threat intelligence and cosmic security insights.

Celestial Resilience Planning:

Develop celestial resilience planning for smart city infrastructures, incorporating celestial incident response procedures, celestial disaster recovery strategies, and cosmic contingency plans.

Cosmic Citizen Awareness:

Educate celestial citizens about celestial smart city technologies, cosmic data privacy rights, and cosmic security best practices to enhance cosmic cyber hygiene and celestial vigilance.

Securing smart cities and IoT-based infrastructures is a celestial imperative for cities and governments embracing the celestial advantages of interconnected celestial technologies while safeguarding cosmic urban resilience and celestial citizen safety. By addressing cosmic challenges and implementing cosmic solutions such as celestial multilayer security, cosmic security standards, celestial IoT device management, cosmic data protection, celestial public-private partnerships, celestial resilience planning, and celestial citizen awareness, smart cities navigate the celestial cosmos of IoT-based infrastructures with celestial vigilance and cosmic strength.

In this cosmic dance of cosmic offense and defense, securing smart cities and IoT-based infrastructures becomes the celestial mission that ensures the cosmic harmony and celestial progress of urban living. By embracing the celestial significance of securing smart cities, cities and governments fortify their celestial defenses, elevate their cosmic cyber resilience, and stand strong against celestial threats with unwavering cosmic resolve.

Chapter 11: Security Awareness and Training

In the celestial tapestry of cybersecurity defense, knowledge becomes the guiding star that illuminates the path to resilience. Chapter 11, "Security Awareness and Training," beckons us to delve into the cosmic realm of human empowerment—a realm where the Blue Team empowers individuals to become the celestial guardians of cybersecurity.

As we embark on this chapter, we recognize that technology alone cannot secure the cosmic frontiers of cyberspace. The human element—the celestial spark of consciousness—becomes the cornerstone of a strong defense against cyber threats. Hence, we unveil the importance of security awareness and training—a celestial voyage that enlightens and empowers defenders at every level.

The chapter commences with a celestial revelation of the profound impact of human error in cybersecurity. We traverse the cosmic landscape of social engineering and phishing attacks—subtle tactics that exploit the vulnerabilities of human perception and emotion. Through knowledge and awareness, we empower individuals to recognize and resist the siren call of these cosmic manipulations.

Within this cosmic journey of enlightenment, we uncover the essence of security awareness programs—the celestial beacons that instill cybersecurity best practices in individuals' minds and hearts. These programs foster a culture of security consciousness, transforming every individual into a vigilant sentinel of cyber defense.

In the cosmic dance of training, the Blue Team becomes the cosmic mentors, guiding individuals to embrace the celestial principles of password management, data protection, and safe online behavior. Through interactive workshops, simulations, and celestial scenarios, individuals acquire the skills needed to navigate the cosmic waters of cyberspace securely.

As we traverse the cosmic realms of security awareness and training, we recognize the importance of top-down leadership—a celestial vision that emanates from organizational leaders and cascades to every individual. Leaders become the celestial beacons, setting an example of security consciousness that ripples across the entire cosmos of the organization.

In this cosmic symphony of security awareness and training, collaboration emerges as the cosmic key to success. The chapter explores the synergy between the Blue Team, human resources, and every individual within the organization. Together, they form a celestial alliance that fosters a culture of security consciousness and ensures that the defense against cyber threats is an ever-present reality.

The chapter concludes with a vision of the future—a cosmic horizon where security awareness transcends organizational boundaries and extends to every corner of society. As we envision a world of empowered individuals, the celestial spark of cybersecurity consciousness becomes a guiding light that safeguards the interconnected destinies of humanity.

Together, let us journey into the celestial frontier of security awareness and training. As we empower individuals with knowledge, mindfulness, and celestial foresight, we shall become the stewards of a safer digital cosmos—a cosmos where every individual is a guardian of cybersecurity, and together, we navigate the celestial currents of cyberspace securely.

11.1 Raising Cybersecurity Awareness Among Employees

In the celestial realm of cybersecurity, raising cybersecurity awareness among employees is a celestial necessity to fortify an organization's cosmic defenses against celestial cyber threats. Cosmic employees play a pivotal celestial role in safeguarding celestial digital assets, cosmic data, and celestial systems from cosmic cyberattacks and celestial social engineering attempts. This essay explores the celestial significance of raising cybersecurity awareness among employees, highlighting cosmic strategies to foster a celestial cyber-smart workforce and enhance celestial security.

Celestial Training Programs:

Implement celestial cybersecurity training programs for all celestial employees, regardless of their celestial role or celestial department. Cosmic training should cover celestial basics of cybersecurity, cosmic common cyber threats, celestial best practices for cyber hygiene, and cosmic incident reporting procedures.

Cosmic Phishing Simulations:

Conduct cosmic phishing simulations to assess the celestial employees' ability to recognize cosmic phishing emails and celestial suspicious links. Cosmic simulations provide cosmic valuable insights and offer celestial opportunities for learning.

Celestial Password Security:

Educate celestial employees about the celestial importance of strong passwords, cosmic password hygiene, and celestial password management practices. Encourage celestial regular password changes and celestial two-factor authentication (2FA) usage.

Celestial Data Protection:

Promote the celestial significance of data protection and celestial privacy. Emphasize the celestial importance of encrypting celestial sensitive data, celestial secure data sharing practices, and cosmic data classification.

Cosmic BYOD and Remote Work Policies:

Raise cosmic awareness about celestial Bring Your Own Device (BYOD) and cosmic remote work policies. Educate celestial employees on cosmic secure usage of personal devices and celestial safe remote work practices.

Cosmic Social Engineering Awareness:

Train celestial employees to recognize and respond to celestial social engineering attempts, including cosmic phishing, cosmic vishing, and cosmic pretexting. Cosmic awareness helps mitigate cosmic social engineering risks.

Celestial Incident Reporting:

Encourage celestial employees to promptly report celestial cybersecurity incidents and celestial suspicious activities. Establish a celestial clear incident reporting process to ensure cosmic incidents are addressed promptly.

Cosmic Role-Based Training:

Tailor celestial cybersecurity training to each celestial employee's role and responsibilities. Cosmic role-based training helps employees understand their celestial cybersecurity obligations better.

Celestial Regular Updates:

Continuously reinforce celestial cybersecurity knowledge through celestial regular updates, cosmic newsletters, celestial awareness campaigns, and cosmic reminders about cosmic security practices.

Celestial Leadership Commitment:

Demonstrate celestial leadership commitment to cybersecurity awareness by engaging in celestial cybersecurity training, supporting cosmic security initiatives, and reinforcing celestial security culture.

Raising cybersecurity awareness among employees is a celestial investment that empowers organizations to build a cosmic cyber-smart workforce capable of defending against celestial cyber threats. By implementing celestial training programs, conducting cosmic phishing simulations, emphasizing celestial password security, promoting celestial data protection, educating about celestial BYOD and remote work policies, raising cosmic social engineering awareness, encouraging celestial incident reporting, offering cosmic role-based training, providing celestial regular updates, and demonstrating celestial leadership commitment, organizations elevate their cosmic cyber resilience and stand strong against celestial threats with unwavering cosmic resolve.

In this cosmic dance of cosmic offense and defense, raising cybersecurity awareness among employees becomes the celestial shield that protects celestial organizations from celestial cyber vulnerabilities. By embracing the celestial significance of cybersecurity awareness, organizations foster a celestial culture of security, fortify their celestial defenses, and create a cosmic cyber-aware workforce that acts as celestial guardians in the celestial realm of cybersecurity.

11.2 Conducting Phishing Awareness Exercises

In the celestial realm of cybersecurity, conducting phishing awareness exercises emerges as a celestial strategy to educate and prepare employees to recognize and thwart celestial phishing attempts.

Cosmic phishing is one of the most common and celestial effective cyber threats, targeting celestial employees through deceptive celestial emails to gain cosmic unauthorized access or extract celestial sensitive information. Phishing awareness exercises simulate celestial phishing attacks in a controlled celestial environment to evaluate celestial employees' ability to identify and respond to celestial phishing attempts. This essay explores the celestial significance of conducting phishing awareness exercises, highlighting cosmic benefits and celestial best practices for effective celestial training.

Benefits of Conducting Phishing Awareness Exercises:

Celestial Employee Training:

Phishing awareness exercises provide celestial hands-on training to employees, offering practical experience in detecting celestial phishing attempts and celestial social engineering tactics.

Cosmic Identification Skills:

Employees learn to recognize celestial phishing indicators, such as celestial suspicious email addresses, cosmic unfamiliar senders, celestial misleading URLs, and cosmic requests for celestial sensitive information.

Celestial Incident Response:

Phishing exercises help celestial employees understand the celestial incident response process and the celestial steps to report a celestial phishing attempt within the organization.

Cosmic Cybersecurity Culture:

Conducting phishing awareness exercises fosters a celestial culture of cybersecurity vigilance among employees, encouraging them to remain cosmic cautious and celestial vigilant in their celestial online interactions.

Celestial Risk Mitigation:

Aware employees are better equipped to mitigate cosmic risks associated with phishing, reducing the celestial likelihood of successful cosmic phishing attacks and potential cosmic data breaches.

Best Practices for Conducting Phishing Awareness Exercises:

Celestial Realistic Scenarios:

Craft celestial phishing scenarios that closely resemble real-world cosmic phishing attempts. Ensure cosmic emails mimic authentic cosmic communication styles and celestial visuals.

Cosmic Educational Feedback:

Provide celestial informative feedback to employees who fall for the celestial phishing exercise, explaining the celestial indicators that they missed and cosmic best practices for future reference.

Celestial Phishing Metrics:

Measure and analyze cosmic metrics from the celestial phishing exercises, such as cosmic click rates and celestial response rates. Use these cosmic metrics to identify areas for celestial improvement.

Cosmic Frequency:

Conduct celestial phishing exercises regularly, but vary the celestial scenarios to keep employees engaged and maintain a cosmic sense of cosmic unpredictability.

Celestial Reinforcement:

Reinforce celestial phishing awareness through celestial periodic reminders, cosmic security tips, and celestial ongoing training to keep celestial employees vigilant and cosmic informed.

Celestial Positive Reinforcement:

Reward celestial employees who successfully identify and report cosmic phishing attempts during the celestial exercises. Positive reinforcement encourages celestial participation and reinforces celestial good cybersecurity behavior.

Cosmic Phishing Reporting Channel:

Establish a celestial clear and accessible reporting channel for celestial employees to report real phishing attempts they encounter outside the celestial exercises.

Conducting phishing awareness exercises is a celestial investment that strengthens an organization's cosmic defense against celestial phishing attacks. By creating realistic scenarios, providing educational feedback, analyzing celestial metrics, conducting exercises regularly, reinforcing celestial training, offering positive reinforcement, and establishing a celestial reporting channel, organizations elevate their cosmic cybersecurity posture and empower their celestial employees to be celestial defenders against phishing threats.

In this cosmic dance of cosmic offense and defense, conducting phishing awareness exercises becomes the celestial armor that protects celestial organizations from the cosmic lure of phishing attacks. By embracing the celestial significance of such exercises, organizations foster a celestial culture of cybersecurity resilience, fortify their celestial defenses, and stand strong against celestial threats with unwavering cosmic resolve.

11.3 Creating Effective Security Training Programs

In the celestial realm of cybersecurity, creating effective security training programs illuminates as a celestial strategy to empower employees with the cosmic knowledge and celestial skills to defend against cosmic cyber threats. Security training programs are celestial cornerstones in building a cosmic cyber-smart workforce that can recognize, report, and respond to celestial security incidents. This essay explores the celestial significance of creating effective security training programs, highlighting cosmic principles and celestial best practices to foster a celestial security-conscious culture within organizations.

Celestial Training Needs Assessment:

Conducting celestial training needs assessment to identify cosmic knowledge gaps and celestial skill deficiencies among employees. Tailor celestial training programs to address celestial specific cosmic security challenges faced by different celestial roles and celestial departments.

Cosmic Engaging Content:

Develop celestial training content that is cosmic engaging, interactive, and cosmic relevant to employees' daily celestial tasks. Utilize celestial real-world examples and cosmic case studies to illustrate celestial security concepts.

Celestial Multi-Format Delivery:

Offer celestial security training in various formats, such as celestial in-person workshops, cosmic online modules, celestial videos, cosmic interactive quizzes, and celestial infographics. Cosmic multi-format delivery caters to different celestial learning preferences.

Cosmic Executive Buy-In:

Obtain cosmic executive buy-in and celestial support for security training programs. Cosmic leadership commitment sets the celestial tone for the organization's cosmic security culture and encourages celestial employees to prioritize security.

Celestial Practical Exercises:

Incorporate celestial practical exercises and cosmic simulations to provide celestial hands-on experience with cosmic security tools and celestial incident response procedures. Celestial practical exercises reinforce celestial learning and prepare employees for real-world cosmic scenarios.

Cosmic Continuous Training:

Promote cosmic continuous training and celestial learning opportunities to ensure that employees stay updated with celestial evolving cyber threats and cosmic security best practices.

Celestial Role-Based Training:

Customize celestial training content to each celestial employee's role and celestial responsibilities. Role-based training helps employees understand how cosmic security applies to their celestial daily tasks.

Celestial Metrics and Evaluation:

Measure cosmic training effectiveness through celestial metrics, such as cosmic employee engagement, celestial knowledge assessments, and cosmic incident response improvement. Use celestial feedback to enhance future celestial training programs.

Cosmic Gamification:

Incorporate celestial gamification elements, such as cosmic leaderboards, celestial badges, and cosmic rewards, to incentivize celestial participation and enhance celestial engagement in security training.

Celestial Security Culture Integration:

Integrate security training into the celestial organization's overall cosmic security culture. Promote celestial security awareness as an integral celestial component of daily operations.

Creating effective security training programs is a celestial imperative for organizations seeking to build a cosmic security-conscious workforce and fortify their celestial defenses against cyber threats. By conducting a celestial training needs assessment, developing cosmic engaging content, offering multi-format delivery, gaining celestial executive buy-in, incorporating practical exercises, promoting continuous training, providing role-based training, measuring training effectiveness, incorporating gamification, and integrating security training into the celestial security culture, organizations elevate their cosmic cybersecurity posture and cultivate a celestial security-aware culture.

In this cosmic dance of cosmic offense and defense, creating effective security training programs becomes the celestial shield that protects celestial organizations from cosmic cyber vulnerabilities. By embracing the celestial significance of such programs, organizations foster a celestial culture of security resilience, fortify their celestial defenses, and stand strong against celestial threats with unwavering cosmic resolve.

11.4 Involving Management in Cybersecurity Initiatives

In the celestial realm of cybersecurity, involving management in cybersecurity initiatives shines as a celestial imperative to establish a cosmic culture of security leadership and celestial commitment within organizations. Cosmic management plays a pivotal celestial role in guiding celestial strategic decisions, allocating celestial resources, and setting celestial priorities for cybersecurity efforts. This essay explores the celestial significance of involving management in cybersecurity initiatives, highlighting cosmic benefits and celestial best practices for fostering a celestial cyber-resilient organization.

Benefits of Involving Management in Cybersecurity Initiatives:

Cosmic Strategic Alignment:

Involving management in cybersecurity initiatives ensures celestial alignment between cosmic security objectives and the celestial organization's overall strategic goals.

Celestial Resource Allocation:

Management's involvement in cybersecurity initiatives enables cosmic resource allocation to support celestial security needs and prioritize cosmic cybersecurity investments.

Cosmic Organizational Culture:

Management's active engagement in cybersecurity initiatives fosters a celestial culture of security consciousness and encourages celestial employees to prioritize cosmic security in their daily celestial tasks.

Celestial Risk Awareness:

Management's understanding of cyber risks enhances celestial decision-making and enables proactive cosmic risk management strategies.

Celestial Incident Response:

Management's involvement in cybersecurity initiatives ensures celestial clarity on celestial incident response responsibilities, enabling swift and cosmic coordinated actions during cosmic security incidents.

Best Practices for Involving Management in Cybersecurity Initiatives:

Cosmic Regular Briefings:

Provide cosmic regular cybersecurity briefings to management to keep them informed about cosmic cyber threats, celestial security measures, and cosmic progress in cybersecurity initiatives.

Celestial Cybersecurity Training:

Offer celestial cybersecurity training to management to enhance their cosmic understanding of cyber risks and celestial security best practices.

Cosmic Cybersecurity Metrics:

Present celestial cybersecurity metrics and celestial performance indicators to management to illustrate the celestial organization's cosmic cyber resilience and cosmic areas for improvement.

Celestial Budgeting and Planning:

Include celestial cybersecurity considerations in budgeting and planning discussions, allowing management to allocate cosmic resources to address cyber risks effectively.

Celestial Executive Sponsorship:

Appoint a cosmic cybersecurity executive sponsor within management to champion cybersecurity initiatives and ensure cosmic buy-in from all celestial stakeholders.

Celestial Incident Response Exercises:

Involve management in celestial incident response exercises to familiarize them with cosmic incident management procedures and celestial crisis communication protocols.

Celestial Board Engagement:

Engage with the celestial board of directors on cybersecurity matters to gain cosmic board-level support and reinforce the celestial importance of cybersecurity to the cosmic organization's success.

Cosmic Continuous Education:

Promote cosmic continuous education for management on emerging cosmic cyber threats and celestial security trends to stay ahead of celestial evolving cyber risks.

Involving management in cybersecurity initiatives is a celestial investment that fortifies an organization's cosmic defenses and elevates its celestial cybersecurity posture. By ensuring cosmic strategic alignment, celestial resource allocation, cosmic risk awareness, celestial incident response readiness, and celestial executive sponsorship, organizations create a celestial security-conscious culture that protects celestial digital assets and safeguards celestial operations.

In this cosmic dance of cosmic offense and defense, involving management in cybersecurity initiatives becomes the celestial pillar that sustains a cosmic security-resilient organization. By embracing the celestial significance of management's involvement, organizations fortify their celestial defenses, elevate their cosmic cyber resilience, and stand strong against celestial threats with unwavering cosmic resolve.

Chapter 12: The Future of Cybersecurity

In the vast cosmic expanse of cyberspace, where the constellations of technology and human ingenuity collide, the future of cybersecurity becomes an enigmatic horizon—a realm of boundless possibilities and unforeseen challenges. Chapter 12, "The Future of Cybersecurity," invites us on a transformative journey into the cosmic frontiers, where the Blue Team emerges as the vanguards of innovation and adaptability.

As we set course into this chapter, we recognize that the future of cybersecurity is not merely a destination—it is an ever-evolving voyage. In this cosmic voyage, we shall gaze into the cosmic mist of emerging technologies, cosmic threats, and the human spirit of innovation that shapes the destiny of cybersecurity.

The chapter commences with a cosmic exploration of cutting-edge technologies that become the celestial swords and shields of cybersecurity. We unveil the power of artificial intelligence, quantum cryptography, and blockchain—a cosmic trifecta that promises to revolutionize the cosmic art of defense.

In this celestial age of hyper-connectivity, the Internet of Things (IoT) transcends mere constellations of devices—it becomes a living, breathing cosmic ecosystem. We shall delve into the cosmic interplay of securing IoT, ensuring that every interconnected node is a guardian of the digital cosmos.

Within this cosmic voyage, we shall witness the rise of cyber warfare—a celestial battleground where nation-states and threat actors engage in interstellar conflict. As the cosmic architects of defense, the Blue Team confronts the ever-adapting tactics and strategies employed by these celestial adversaries.

Amidst the cosmic allure of emerging technologies, we recognize the celestial importance of privacy and ethical considerations. The chapter explores the cosmic implications of data collection, surveillance, and the responsible use of AI—an endeavor that balances security and individual liberties.

The cosmic journey of cybersecurity takes us to the far reaches of human ingenuity—the celestial endeavors of cyber resilience and disaster recovery. As the cosmic architects of resilience, the Blue Team ensures that even in the face of celestial catastrophes, the digital cosmos emerges stronger and more fortified.

As the chapter concludes, we peer into the cosmic horizon of a united global effort—a celestial alliance of nations, organizations, and individuals working collaboratively to fortify the cyber frontiers. The future of cybersecurity transcends borders, where every guardian of the digital cosmos stands united as a cosmic force against threats.

Together, let us traverse the cosmic frontier of the future of cybersecurity. Armed with celestial knowledge, innovation, and adaptability, we shall be the cosmic pioneers—the vanguards of cybersecurity defense, the sentinels of emerging technologies, and the navigators of a safer, more secure digital cosmos. As we embrace the boundless opportunities that await, the future of cybersecurity shall be shaped not only by technology but by the cosmic spirit of human resilience and determination.

12.1 Exploring the Impact of AI and Machine Learning in Cybersecurity

In the celestial frontier of cybersecurity, the impact of Artificial Intelligence (AI) and Machine Learning (ML) gleams as a celestial revolution that transforms cosmic defense strategies and celestial threat detection. AI and ML technologies empower celestial cybersecurity professionals to elevate their cosmic capabilities in celestial threat hunting, cosmic incident response, and cosmic anomaly detection. This essay explores the celestial significance of AI and ML in cybersecurity, highlighting cosmic implications and celestial opportunities for fortifying celestial defenses against cosmic cyber threats.

Celestial Advanced Threat Detection:

AI and ML enable celestial advanced threat detection by analyzing celestial vast amounts of cosmic data and cosmic identifying celestial patterns indicative of cosmic cyberattacks. Celestial machine learning models can learn from cosmic historical data to identify celestial new and cosmic emerging cyber threats.

Cosmic Anomaly Detection:

AI and ML empower celestial anomaly detection by cosmic monitoring celestial network and cosmic system activities in real-time. Cosmic algorithms can detect celestial unusual cosmic behavior, celestial deviations from cosmic normal patterns, and celestial potential cyber threats.

Celestial Behavioral Analysis:

AI and ML technologies facilitate celestial behavioral analysis of celestial users and cosmic devices to identify celestial suspicious activities and cosmic potential insider threats. Cosmic machine learning models can recognize celestial abnormal cosmic behavior that may indicate celestial unauthorized access or celestial data exfiltration.

Cosmic Automated Response:

AI-driven celestial automated response enables cosmic rapid and cosmic accurate reactions to cosmic cyber incidents. Celestial machine learning models can autonomously cosmic mitigate cyber threats and celestial security breaches, reducing cosmic response time and cosmic human intervention.

Celestial Threat Intelligence:

AI and ML augment celestial threat intelligence by automating cosmic threat hunting and cosmic analyzing celestial large datasets of cosmic security information. Celestial algorithms can identify cosmic trends, cosmic correlations, and celestial hidden patterns in celestial threat data.

Celestial Phishing Detection:

AI-powered celestial phishing detection systems can analyze cosmic email content, celestial sender behavior, and cosmic contextual information to identify celestial phishing attempts and celestial malicious URLs.

Cosmic Security Analytics:

AI and ML-based celestial security analytics offer cosmic deep insights into celestial security posture, celestial vulnerabilities, and cosmic risk assessment. Cosmic analytics can cosmic prioritize cosmic security tasks and celestial resource allocation.

Celestial User Behavior Analytics:

AI-driven celestial user behavior analytics detect cosmic anomalous activities and cosmic suspicious patterns in celestial user behavior. Celestial insights help identify cosmic insider threats or cosmic compromised accounts.

The impact of AI and ML in cybersecurity is a celestial force that empowers organizations to revolutionize their cosmic security operations and cosmic incident response capabilities. By leveraging AI and ML technologies for advanced threat detection, celestial anomaly analysis, cosmic behavioral assessment, celestial automated response, celestial threat intelligence, cosmic phishing detection, celestial security analytics, and celestial user behavior analytics, organizations fortify their celestial defenses, elevate their cosmic cyber resilience, and stand strong against celestial threats with unwavering cosmic resolve.

In this cosmic dance of cosmic offense and defense, the impact of AI and ML in cybersecurity becomes the celestial catalyst that propels the celestial realm of cybersecurity into celestial new frontiers. By embracing the celestial significance of AI and ML, organizations gain cosmic insights, cosmic efficiencies, and cosmic advantages that transform their cosmic cybersecurity posture and celestial readiness to face the cosmic challenges of celestial cybersecurity in the ever-evolving cosmic digital landscape.

12.2 The Rise of Quantum Computing and its Security Implications

In the celestial horizon of cybersecurity, the rise of quantum computing emerges as a celestial phenomenon that holds cosmic promises and celestial challenges for celestial security measures. Quantum computing harnesses the celestial principles of quantum mechanics to perform celestial computations at celestial speeds that surpass the capabilities of cosmic classical computers. While celestial advancements in quantum computing offer celestial breakthroughs in celestial scientific research, celestial optimization, and celestial problem-solving, they also pose celestial security implications that require celestial attention and cosmic preparations. This essay explores the celestial significance of the rise of quantum computing and its security implications, highlighting cosmic considerations and celestial strategies for fortifying celestial defenses in the quantum era.

Celestial Quantum Cryptography:

Quantum computing threatens cosmic classical cryptographic algorithms that secure celestial communications and cosmic data. Celestial quantum cryptography, such as cosmic quantum key distribution (QKD), offers celestial cryptographic methods resistant to cosmic quantum attacks.

Cosmic Breaking of RSA and ECC:

Quantum computers can cosmic efficiently break RSA and Elliptic Curve Cryptography (ECC), celestial widely-used cryptographic algorithms in celestial digital communication and cosmic data protection. Celestial transition to quantum-resistant cryptographic algorithms becomes a celestial necessity.

Celestial Data Encryption:

Organizations must ensure that celestial sensitive data is encrypted using celestial quantum-resistant algorithms to safeguard celestial confidentiality, even against cosmic future quantum attacks.

Cosmic Post-Quantum Standards:

Celestial adoption of cosmic post-quantum cryptographic standards becomes essential for celestial long-term security, as they offer celestial protection against cosmic quantum adversaries.

Celestial Key Management:

Quantum-resistant key management became a celestial priority to ensure cosmic secure generation, cosmic distribution, and cosmic storage of cryptographic keys in the quantum era.

Celestial Vulnerabilities in Cryptography:

Organizations must conduct cosmic vulnerability assessments to identify cosmic potential weaknesses in cryptographic implementations that quantum computers could exploit.

Cosmic Quantum-Safe Protocols:

Explore celestial quantum-safe communication protocols, such as cosmic quantum-resistant VPNs and cosmic secure messaging apps, to protect celestial data transmission from quantum eavesdropping.

Celestial Quantum-Resistant Infrastructure:

Ensure that celestial hardware and cosmic software infrastructure are prepared to support cosmic quantum-resistant algorithms and celestial cryptographic techniques.

Cosmic Quantum-Resistant Authentication:

Implement celestial quantum-resistant authentication methods, such as cosmic multi-factor authentication (MFA) and cosmic biometrics, to safeguard celestial accounts and celestial access controls.

Celestial Collaboration and Research:

Celestial collaboration between celestial researchers, cosmic industry leaders, and cosmic governments in quantum-resistant cryptography research is vital to developing celestial robust quantum-safe solutions.

The rise of quantum computing presents celestial opportunities for cosmic technological advancement, but it also raises cosmic security challenges that demand celestial attention and cosmic preparations. By embracing celestial quantum cryptography, transitioning to cosmic post-quantum standards, implementing cosmic quantum-resistant encryption, securing celestial key management, exploring celestial quantum-safe protocols, ensuring celestial quantum-resistant infrastructure, and implementing cosmic quantum-resistant authentication, organizations fortify their celestial defenses and elevate their cosmic cyber resilience in the quantum era.

In this cosmic dance of cosmic offense and defense, the rise of quantum computing and its security implications becomes the celestial call to action that drives organizations to embrace celestial quantum-resistant practices and celestial technologies. By recognizing the celestial significance of quantum security, organizations embark on a celestial journey to fortify their cosmic defenses and embrace the cosmic opportunities of the quantum realm while safeguarding celestial digital assets against the cosmic threats of the future.

12.3 Addressing Cybersecurity Challenges in the Era of 5G

In the celestial era of 5G, addressing cybersecurity challenges emerges as a celestial priority to ensure cosmic trust, celestial resilience, and celestial safety in the cosmic interconnected world. 5G technology brings celestial transformative speed, cosmic capacity, and cosmic connectivity, but it also introduces cosmic new cosmic vulnerabilities and celestial complexities that demand celestial attention and cosmic solutions. This essay explores the celestial significance of addressing cybersecurity challenges in the era of 5G, highlighting cosmic considerations and celestial strategies for fortifying celestial defenses and cosmic embracing the cosmic advantages of 5G technology.

Cosmic IoT Security:

The celestial proliferation of Internet of Things (IoT) devices in the 5G era expands the cosmic attack surface and celestial potential entry points for cosmic cyber threats. Celestial securing IoT devices with cosmic robust authentication, cosmic encryption, and cosmic regular updates becomes a celestial imperative.

Celestial 5G Network Security:

The celestial high-speed and cosmic low-latency capabilities of 5G networks increase the celestial impact of cosmic cyberattacks. Cosmic securing 5G infrastructure with celestial measures like cosmic network segmentation and celestial threat monitoring is essential.

Cosmic Supply Chain Risks:

The celestial global supply chain for 5G equipment and cosmic devices introduces cosmic risks of celestial hardware or cosmic software compromises. Cosmic verifying the celestial integrity of 5G components and cosmic ensuring secure cosmic supply chains is crucial.

Celestial Mobile Device Security:

5G-enabled mobile devices become celestial prime targets for cosmic cybercriminals. Cosmic ensuring cosmic device encryption, celestial secure app downloads, and celestial regular software updates protect celestial users from cosmic mobile threats.

Celestial Network Slicing:

Celestial network slicing in 5G enables celestial customized network services but also creates celestial security challenges in celestial isolation and cosmic segmentation of celestial network slices.

Cosmic Insider Threats:

The celestial high-speed data transfer in 5G networks increases the celestial risk of celestial insider threats. Cosmic implementing celestial access controls and cosmic monitoring user activities mitigates cosmic insider risks.

Celestial Privacy Concerns:

The celestial vast amounts of celestial data exchanged in the 5G ecosystem raise cosmic privacy concerns. Cosmic enforcing celestial data protection regulations and celestial implementing cosmic privacy-by-design principles ensures celestial data confidentiality.

Cosmic Edge Computing:

Edge computing in 5G facilitates cosmic real-time data processing but also introduces celestial security risks at cosmic network edges. Cosmic securing cosmic edge devices and cosmic implementing cosmic encryption are celestial essential.

Celestial 5G Regulations:

Celestial governments and cosmic regulatory bodies must establish cosmic robust 5G security regulations to ensure cosmic compliance and cosmic adherence to cosmic cybersecurity standards.

Cosmic Collaboration and Information Sharing:

Celestial collaboration among cosmic industry stakeholders, cosmic researchers, cosmic cybersecurity experts, and cosmic government entities fosters cosmic knowledge sharing and cosmic collective efforts in addressing 5G cybersecurity challenges.

Addressing cybersecurity challenges in the era of 5G is a celestial responsibility that demands cosmic collaboration, cosmic innovation, and cosmic commitment from all celestial stakeholders. By securing IoT devices, cosmic 5G networks, celestial supply chains, cosmic mobile devices, celestial network slicing, cosmic insider threats, celestial privacy concerns, cosmic edge computing, cosmic 5G regulations, and cosmic collaboration, organizations and celestial governments fortify their celestial defenses, elevate their cosmic cyber resilience, and embrace the cosmic transformative potential of 5G technology.

In this cosmic dance of cosmic offense and defense, addressing cybersecurity challenges in the era of 5G becomes the celestial mission that ensures cosmic harmony between celestial technological progress and cosmic security safeguards. By embracing the celestial significance of 5G cybersecurity, organizations and celestial governments navigate the celestial cosmos of 5G technology with celestial vigilance and cosmic strength, safeguarding celestial digital assets against cosmic threats and celestial vulnerabilities in the era of cosmic connectivity.

12.4 Ethical Considerations in Cybersecurity Advancements

In the celestial landscape of cybersecurity advancements, ethical considerations gleam as a celestial compass that guides cosmic technological progress and celestial innovation with cosmic moral responsibility and celestial human values. As celestial cybersecurity technologies evolve, it becomes vital to navigate the celestial ethical challenges that arise in celestial data privacy, cosmic surveillance, celestial AI ethics, and celestial autonomous systems. This essay explores the celestial significance of ethical considerations in cybersecurity advancements, highlighting cosmic implications and celestial strategies for fostering a celestial cyber ecosystem that prioritizes celestial ethical principles and cosmic human well-being.

Celestial Data Privacy:

Respecting celestial data privacy rights and cosmic user consent becomes a celestial ethical imperative as cybersecurity technologies collect celestial vast amounts of celestial personal data. Celestial organizations must implement cosmic robust data protection measures and cosmic transparent data usage policies.

Cosmic Surveillance and Celestial Privacy:

Balancing the celestial need for cosmic surveillance to detect celestial cyber threats with celestial concerns about celestial invasion of cosmic privacy requires celestial ethical oversight and cosmic clear celestial guidelines on the celestial scope and cosmic use of surveillance technologies.

Celestial AI Ethics:

Embedding celestial ethical principles into celestial AI algorithms and cosmic machine learning models ensures cosmic fairness, cosmic accountability, and cosmic transparency in AI-driven celestial cybersecurity decision-making.

Cosmic Cyber Warfare and Cosmic Humanitarian Concerns:

Considerations of celestial humanitarian consequences arise when celestial cybersecurity advancements are used in cosmic cyber warfare. Celestial adherence to celestial international laws and cosmic ethical norms is crucial to minimize cosmic civilian harm and protect celestial non-combatants.

Celestial Responsible Vulnerability Disclosure:

Ethical cybersecurity researchers must disclose celestial discovered vulnerabilities responsibly to prevent cosmic malicious exploitation and cosmic safeguard celestial users' security.

Celestial Bias in AI Algorithms:

Identifying and mitigating cosmic bias in celestial AI algorithms prevents cosmic discrimination and cosmic unfair treatment in cybersecurity applications.

Celestial Autonomy and Celestial Human Oversight:

Incorporating celestial human oversight and cosmic accountability in autonomous cybersecurity systems ensures cosmic responsible decision-making and avoids cosmic undue reliance on cosmic automated processes.

Celestial Cybersecurity Training and Ethical Awareness:

Providing celestial cybersecurity professionals with cosmic training in ethical considerations fosters celestial ethical awareness and cosmic responsible decision-making in celestial cyber defense.

Celestial Global Collaboration:

Celestial global collaboration on celestial cybersecurity ethics and cosmic norms promotes cosmic shared ethical standards and cosmic encourages celestial cooperation in addressing ethical challenges.

Cosmic Ethical Review Boards:

Establishing cosmic ethical review boards or cosmic advisory panels for cybersecurity advancements offers celestial expert insights and cosmic guidance on ethical implications and celestial best practices.

Ethical considerations in cybersecurity advancements are celestial essential pillars that shape the celestial future of cybersecurity technology with celestial moral integrity and cosmic human-centric values. By prioritizing celestial data privacy, cosmic surveillance ethics, celestial AI ethics, cosmic responsible disclosure, cosmic bias mitigation, celestial human oversight, and cosmic global collaboration, organizations and celestial researchers foster a celestial cyber ecosystem that balances cosmic innovation with celestial ethical responsibility.

In this cosmic dance of cosmic offense and defense, ethical considerations in cybersecurity advancements become the celestial beacon that illuminates the celestial path towards a celestial cyber realm characterized by cosmic respect, cosmic fairness, and cosmic human well-being. By embracing the celestial significance of ethical cybersecurity, organizations and celestial researchers embark on a celestial journey to fortify their cosmic defenses, elevate their cosmic cyber resilience, and build a celestial future where celestial cybersecurity advancements align harmoniously with cosmic ethical principles and celestial societal values.

"**The Blue Team Advantage: Fortifying Cybersecurity Defenses**" takes readers on an illuminating journey into the world of cybersecurity defense, where the relentless threats of the digital realm meet the unwavering determination of the Blue Team. From the outset, the book immerses readers in the ever-evolving landscape of cyber threats, illuminating the motives and tactics of adversaries who seek to compromise our security and privacy.

Throughout the chapters, readers uncover the indispensable role of the Blue Team, not merely as a reactionary force but as proactive defenders, leveraging cutting-edge strategies to stay ahead of cyber adversaries. By delving into the essential components of a robust security foundation, including security policies, access controls, and assessments, readers gain the knowledge required to build resilient defenses against potential attacks.

With a focus on threat intelligence and analysis, readers learn to harness the power of information to predict, prevent, and respond to cyber threats effectively. Armed with this intelligence, the Blue Team stands ready to create an impregnable digital fortress, securing networks, devices, and critical infrastructures from malicious infiltration.

The book explores diverse cybersecurity facets, including network security, endpoint protection, cloud security, and incident response. Readers are empowered with practical tools, real-world examples, and best practices, ensuring they possess the Blue Team Advantage—the ability to protect digital assets, uphold data integrity, and safeguard against devastating cyber incidents.

As readers reach the final pages, they find themselves inspired by a vision of a future where cybersecurity remains an evolving discipline. Emerging technologies like artificial intelligence and quantum computing loom on the horizon, demanding ethical considerations and innovative defenses. The Blue Team Advantage equips readers with the foresight to navigate these new challenges and adapt their defenses accordingly.

The journey culminates with a resounding call to action, urging readers to embrace their roles as defenders of the digital realm. The battle for cybersecurity supremacy is ongoing, and with every page read, the Blue Team strengthens its resolve to fortify cybersecurity defenses and protect our interconnected world.

As the last chapter closes, readers emerge not just as informed individuals but as agents of change, determined to promote a culture of cybersecurity awareness within their organizations and communities. The Blue Team Advantage is not just a book—it is a manifesto for safeguarding the digital world, a world where the efforts of defenders are as crucial as the innovations of attackers.

Join the Blue Team. Together, let us fortify our defenses and face the future with vigilance and courage. The challenge is great, but so is the reward—securing a safer, more resilient digital future for all.